Death and the Maiden

A Play

Georgina Reid

Samuel French – London
New York – Sydney – Toronto – Hollywood

CHARACTERS

Mrs Bell
Mavis Bell, her daughter
Ellen
Sylvia Morley, Mrs Bell's daughter
Rose Morley, Sylvia's daughter
Dr Parry
Arthur Fox

The action takes place in the parlour at Gorse Cottage

Period—the beginning of the twentieth century

ACT·I   SCENE 1   A Saturday afternoon in September
         SCENE 2   Saturday morning, a week later
         SCENE 3   That afternoon, about five o'clock

ACT II   That evening, about six-thirty. During the scene the Lights are lowered briefly to indicate the passage of one hour

ACT I*

Scene 1

The parlour at Gorse Cottage. A Saturday afternoon in September at the beginning of the twentieth century

There is a door upstage centre to the hall, and a full-length glass door to the garden R *(open). There is a window in the wall* L. *By the fireside* DL *are an armchair and a low stool. There is a sideboard* UR *and a sofa* DR. *There are two lamps*

There is no fire burning and the room is bright with September sunshine

Mrs Bell is dozing in the armchair. She is about seventy-five and is rather frail. She suffers from arthritis and walks with the aid of a stick. She also has a very bad heart

After a moment Ellen comes through the garden door. She is seventeen and very pretty in a conventional sort of way. She is carrying a life-like toy cat in her arms

Ellen Mrs Bell! Mrs Bell! I've brought a visitor to see you. He's called Felix.

She perches the cat on Mrs Bell's knees. Mrs Bell opens her eyes. At the sight of the cat she screams loudly in terror

Mrs Bell Take it away! Don't let it come near me! Oh! Oh!

She continues to scream feebly while Ellen takes the cat and runs out again into the garden

At the same time, Mavis Bell runs in from the hall. She is fifty years old, grey-haired and thin. She looks tired and depressed

Mavis Mother, what is it?
Mrs Bell A cat! A huge black cat!
Mavis (*looking round*) Where? I don't see it.
Mrs Bell It was Ellen. She brought it in.

Mavis goes and looks out into the garden

Her mother struggles to her feet and makes for the door

Don't let her bring it back. Oh my heart. Oh dear. I need my smelling salts.

She goes out, moaning

Ellen re-appears at the garden door, without the cat

Mavis Ellen, you gave my mother an awful shock. She's terrified of cats.
Ellen I'm ever so sorry, Miss Bell. It wasn't a real one, you know. Can't she see very well?
Mavis No, of course not, at her age. Whatever were you thinking of?
Ellen I had no idea it would upset her so.
Mavis Her heart is very bad.
Ellen Can I do anything?
Mavis Yes. I'd be glad if you'd fetch the doctor.
Ellen From his surgery?
Mavis No. From the cornfield.
Ellen The cornfield?
Mavis (*pointing towards the garden*) Doctor Parry is over there, helping the reapers in the cornfield. Run and get him please.

Ellen runs out quickly

Mavis goes to sideboard and gets pills and a glass of water

Mrs Bell peers round the door

Mrs Bell Has she gone?
Mavis Yes.

Mrs Bell comes in holding some smelling salts to her nose

Come and sit down, Mother. I think you'd better take a pill, to calm your heart.
Mrs Bell (*sitting*) It needs more than doctor's pills to mend this creaking piece of machinery.
Mavis I know, but pills are better than nothing. You don't want to be poorly when Sylvia arrives.
Mrs Bell (*acidly*) No, and *you* don't want me poorly just now, or you won't be able to go off on your holiday. No wonder you're so solicitous all of a sudden. (*She takes two pills, with water*)

Mavis restores box of pills and glass of water to the sideboard

Wretched pills. They always stick in my throat and the taste is awful.
Mavis How are you feeling now?
Mrs Bell Dreadful.
Mavis You look very pale.
Mrs Bell So do you. The trouble with *you*, Mavis, is that you don't know how to look pale and interesting.
Mavis I think you must be feeling better, Mother.
Mrs Bell Huh! I'm not going to die just yet, thank you. I'll die when it suits my convenience and not yours, my girl. At the moment I have other

things to think about. I've looked forward to this day for twenty years and I intend to be fit to enjoy it.

Mavis Is it really twenty years since Sylvia left home?

Mrs Bell All but a few months. I hope you'll be nice to her when she arrives.

Mavis Nice to her? I shall be overjoyed. I love Sylvia.

Mrs Bell You never used to. You were always jealous of her.

Mavis Jealous? Never.

Mrs Bell I don't like to be contradicted, Mavis. I said jealous and I meant it. You were jealous of all the things she had that you couldn't hope for . . . beauty, admiration, a husband, a baby . . .

Mavis Mother, it would be useless to deny that I envied her, but I never stopped loving her. Who could help it?

Mrs Bell Who, indeed! She was the most adorable girl. I hope she hasn't changed in all those years abroad.

Dr Parry appears at the garden door. He is an attractive young man in his twenties. He is in his shirt sleeves and looks hot and ruddy

Mrs Bell puts on an expression of gentle sweetness and looks up at him appealingly. In the presence of a man she automatically blossoms

Dr Parry Am I needed? Ellen said you'd sent for me.

Mavis Yes. My mother had rather a nasty shock and her heart is giving trouble.

Mrs Bell My silly old ticker, up to its old tricks again, Doctor.

Dr Parry And what was this nasty shock?

Mavis It was that naughty girl, Ellen, from next door.

Mrs Bell Oh, you mustn't blame Ellen. She didn't know that I'm afraid of cats.

Dr Parry And Ellen brought a cat in, did she?

Mrs Bell Yes, and when I saw it I screamed so loud, the poor girl thought I'd gone mad.

Mavis She spends too much time hanging about this house. I've a good mind to speak to her mother.

Mrs Bell (*gently*) Oh no, don't do that, Mavis. I love to see her pretty face peeping in at the window. We old fogies don't see enough young people.

Dr Parry I'll just take your pulse if I may, Mrs Bell.

She gives him her hand

I hope you'll forgive my shirt sleeves. I've been working in the cornfield, just for a bit of fun.

Mavis Yes, we saw you.

Mrs Bell We could hardly believe our eyes. A doctor working side by side with the reapers. Is that your idea of fun?

Dr Parry Yes. I spend so much of my life sitting by people's bedsides that when I have a few hours off, I like to be outside, working hard, surrounded by healthy people.

Mrs Bell Goodness, if you're that fond of exercise, you can come and cut our grass for us. It's too high to walk in and we can't get a man to come.

Mavis How do you think Mother's heart is, Dr Parry?

Dr Parry It's none too steady but I think she'll be all right. Not too much excitement, please.

Mrs Bell That's a vain hope, Doctor. You don't realize that today something *very* exciting is due to happen. At any moment now in fact. My daughter Sylvia is coming home. She's been in Ceylon for twenty years!

Dr Parry Twenty years! It's going to be quite a reunion.

Mavis And she's bringing her daughter Rose.

Mrs Bell Rose must be quite grown up by now. How old will she be, Mavis?

Mavis Eighteen, Mother.

Mrs Bell Eighteen ... just fancy! On the brink of womanhood and as enchanting as her mother I don't doubt. Won't she turn a few heads in the village? You'd better look in, later on, Dr Parry—find some excuse—and I'll introduce you to my beautiful granddaughter.

Dr Parry How long will they be staying?

Mrs Bell Just for a week. They're going to look after me while Mavis is away at Cheltenham.

Dr Parry Your annual holiday, Miss Bell?

Mavis Yes. I shan't see a lot of my sister and niece, I'm afraid. As soon as they arrive I shall have to leave. But later on, when they've settled in their new house, we're both invited to visit them.

Mrs Bell If I'm fit to go, that is. My wretched health casts such a blight on things. I wonder poor Mavis doesn't lose patience with me. (*She smiles up at Mavis and pats her hand*) But she needs a holiday and this week she shall have it. You mustn't worry about me, dear, while you're in Cheltenham. I shall be all right with Sylvia and Rose. We'll have quite a gay time, I expect.

Dr Parry Well, I must be going. Try and take things quietly, Mrs Bell. And I hope *you'll* have a gay time, too, Miss Mavis, at Cheltenham. (*He goes to the garden door*)

Mavis Thank you, Doctor. I'll try but I haven't much talent for gaiety.

Dr Parry exits

Mrs Bell (*sourly*) And that's the truest word you've spoken today. In all the years I've known you—and that's nearly fifty—I've never seen an expression of gaiety cross your earnest face. Do you realize that I called you Mavis because it's the name of a *bird*—a thrush or something—and I hoped you would sing. But not you. Singing is what joyful people do.

Mavis I sang in the choir until you ... persuaded me not to.

Mrs Bell I did that to save your dignity. If you hadn't left of your own accord, they'd have asked you to go. You never had an ear for music. Whenever I came to church I could hear you up there in the choir, singing out of tune. I used to go hot and cold with shame. Then in the end the choirmaster came to see me and begged me to persuade you to give it up.

Mavis gets up with a blank face

Where are you going?

Mavis I've to finish my packing.

Mrs Bell That's right. Pack all your finery. You'll want to impress the citizens of Cheltenham.

Mavis On the contrary. I expect to have a very quiet week with Bertha.

Mrs Bell Then you might as well not go. Mavis, I despair of you. Surely you'll have a few outings. You'll be going to the theatre?

Mavis Perhaps. And a concert, I expect.

Mrs Bell That's better. That reminds me. I want you to fetch me my jewel box from my dressing table.

Mavis Mother ... I ...

Mrs Bell Go on. It won't take you a minute.

Mavis hurries out

Mrs Bell goes and peers out of the window, right, admiring the view

Mavis returns carrying the jewel box

Mrs Bell Look at those reapers, how strong they are. Doesn't it do you good to watch them?

Mavis Mother ... you asked for your jewel box.

Mrs Bell Ah yes. Take out my emerald brooch.

Mavis The one Father gave you? (*She takes it out and gives it to Mrs Bell*)

Mrs Bell Yes. Now Mavis, I want you to have this.

Mavis Oh, no. I couldn't. It's far too precious.

Mrs Bell Yes, yes, you could and you shall. It will look very good on your dress when you go to a concert. Bertha will be quite envious.

Mavis I'll borrow it then.

Mrs Bell No, no, it's yours. I have other good brooches. I can spare this one for you. Keep it, dear, as a little present from your mother.

Mavis I ... well ... thank you very much. It's very kind of you.

Mrs Bell Don't I get a kiss?

Mavis Of course.

She gives her mother a peck, then pins the brooch on her dress. Then the sound of wheels is heard

Mrs Bell Listen! Is that the carriage?

They go to the window, L

Mavis It is! It's them! It must be! Yes, I can see Sylvia getting out!

Mrs Bell Oh, my heart! It's jumping about all over the place.

Mavis You sit down. I'll let them in.

She runs out

Mrs Bell sits on chair facing the door, tense and eager, hand pressed to her heart

Sylvia (*off*) Mavis! Darling Mavis! Isn't this wonderful?

Mavis (*off*) Sylvia! Oh my dear girl, after all these years.

Sylvia (*off*) Where's Mother?

Mavis (*off*) In the parlour.

Sylvia runs in, a pretty, vivacious woman of forty-three

Mrs Bell struggles to her feet and opens her arms. Sylvia embraces her fervently

Sylvia Mother! At last!

Mrs Bell Oh my darling girl! My beautiful daughter!

Sylvia How could I stay away so long? How can you ever forgive me?

Mrs Bell I can forgive you anything. Let me look at you. Still so lovely. Still so young and fascinating. If ever there was a sight for sore eyes, you are.

Sylvia Mother, you're trembling.

Mrs Bell It's my heart, dear.

Sylvia Sit down.

Sylvia seats her in chair DL

Mrs Bell It's all right. Just the excitement.

Sylvia I know. We're excited, too. Rose could hardly sit still.

Mrs Bell Where is she, your little Rose?

Sylvia She's talking to Mavis. And she's *not* so little. Rose! Here's Grandma!

Rose enters. She stands in the doorway and there is a moment's silence as they look at her

Mrs Bell's disappointment is plain

Rose has none of her mother's beauty. She is thin and wears glasses. Her hair is cut short and her complexion is sallow. Nevertheless, she has charm and grace and an underlying strength of character

Mavis stands beside her

Rose Hello, Grandmother.

Mrs Bell So this is Rose.

Sylvia Well, give her a kiss, child. You've come thousands of miles to do it, so let's see it happen.

Rose bends over Mrs Bell and kisses her

Mrs Bell Come and sit on this stool so that I can look at you.

Rose sits on low stool by the fire

Rose I'm afraid I come as a bit of a disappointment after Mother.

Mrs Bell You certainly aren't much like Sylvia, it's true. You must take after your father's side of the family.

Rose No, honestly I don't. It's all highly suspicious. We think Mother must have had a scandalous past.

Sylvia (*laughing*) Rose! Darling! Somebody might take you seriously.

Mrs Bell You do remind me of somebody, though.

Sylvia Of course she does. She's Mavis all over again.

Mavis Oh, surely not.

Sylvia Yes, when you were her age you were very similar. I've a photograph taken at my tenth birthday. You'd just started wearing spectacles and you hated them.

Rose Do you still hate them, Aunt Mavis?

Mavis Yes. I ... I only wear them for reading. It's vanity, I suppose.

Rose Oh, do put them on and then we'll be twins.

Rose jumps up and goes to Mavis

Sylvia You can take the baggage upstairs—and my hat. (*She gives her hat to Rose*)

Mavis I'll show you your bedroom. It's very small, I'm afraid.

Rose Never mind, I can always stick my legs up the chimney.

Mavis (*smiling*) Like Alice in Wonderland.

Rose and Mavis exit, talking

Sylvia I can see they're going to get on like a house on fire.

Mrs Bell (*without enthusiasm*) Yes, she's a nice girl, but ... what have you done to her hair?

Sylvia (*laughing*) I didn't do it. Rose cut it off herself. She said it was too hot.

Mrs Bell And her complexion. She looks so *brown*.

Sylvia I know. She's spent so much of her life in the open air and she just won't wear a hat or carry a parasol. Honestly, Mother, if she wore a sari, you'd take her for one of the natives!

Mrs Bell I can believe that. But Sylvia, now you're in England, she can't go round looking like a native of Ceylon.

Sylvia Don't worry, Mother. Her hair will grow. Her tan will fade. In six months' time you won't know her.

Mrs Bell I wonder. She's remarkably like Mavis.

Sylvia Well, isn't that nice? You ought to be pleased.

Mrs Bell (*temper breaking out*) But I wanted her to be like *you*! I *counted* on her being like you!

Sylvia Mother, Mavis hasn't a daughter of her own. Don't you think it's nice that her niece takes after her?

Mrs Bell (*scathingly*) Mavis wasn't cut out for motherhood. She was born to be a maiden aunt.

Sylvia (*with a sigh*) Poor Mavis (*She looks round admiringly*) Isn't this a pretty room, and haven't you got some lovely views! Oh, that great yellow field of corn—and the beautiful oak trees. When I see oak trees like that I know I'm in England again.

Mrs Bell And you're going to stay?

Sylvia Yes. Peter finally decided his daughter must come home and learn to be an English lady.

Mrs Bell What about the tea plantation?

Sylvia He sold it. Made a big profit, I'm glad to say. Enough to buy a small estate in Suffolk. We'll be settled in by Christmas and you must both come and stay. It'll be wonderful.

Mrs Bell And you'll wear pretty dresses and jewellery, and there'll be music and dancing and laughing and singing ...

Sylvia I hope so. I like the sound of that.

Mrs Bell Yes, the kind of life you were born for, my darling. I'm afraid you'll be terribly bored here, for a whole week.

Sylvia Nonsense. I'm never bored as long as Rose is with me.

Mrs Bell Oh.

Sylvia (*seeing her mistake*) And *you*, dear. How could I be bored when I have you for company? We'll have so much to say, we shan't draw breath for a week. Every morning we'll walk round the garden—can you walk that far?

Mrs Bell If we go slowly.

Sylvia We'll be a couple of tortoises. And in the evening we'll play rummy. Rummy is the only card game I know. You taught me how to play that, do you remember? And when we're sick of rummy we'll play Halma. Have you still got the Halma board?

Mrs Bell I think so. I must ask Mavis where it is.

Mavis and Rose enter

Mavis, have we still got the Halma board?

Mavis Gracious, no. The pieces got lost and the board fell apart ages ago.

Sylvia I'll buy you another for Christmas. I want to be the Halma champion again.

Rose Mother, I've unpacked our presents. (*She hands a wrapped object to Sylvia*)

Sylvia Oh yes, a present for you, Mother, from Ceylon. (*She hands it to Mrs Bell*)

Mrs Bell unwraps a carved wooden figure

It's done by native craftsmen out of local wood.

Mrs Bell How remarkable. Look, Mavis, isn't that a fine piece of work?

Mavis Beautiful.

Mrs Bell (*to Sylvia*) Thank you, dear. I shall treasure it.

Sylvia And Rose has a gift for you. One she made herself.

Rose It's a shawl.

She hands Mrs Bell a parcel. Mrs Bell unwraps a crocheted shawl

Mrs Bell Oh, very nice. Thank you dear.

Rose I made one for you, too, Auntie. (*She gives Mavis a similar parcel*)

Mavis (*unwrapping it*) Oh, how lovely! You clever girl! Look, Mother, to think of Rose making these for us. It must have taken ages.

Rose Quite a while.

Mrs Bell I hope you didn't strain your eyesight doing this.

Rose Oh no. I enjoyed doing it, honestly.

Mavis And I shall enjoy wearing it, dear. I shall take it to Cheltenham and flaunt it at the theatre.

Sylvia Try it on, Mother. Let's see if the colour suits you.

Rose Yes, please try it on, Grandma.

Mrs Bell I'll do it in my room, where I can look at myself in the long mirror.

She goes to the door, taking her jewel box with her

Rose May I come too?

Rose and Mrs Bell go out together

Sylvia Can she manage the stairs?

Mavis She sleeps downstairs. Her room is just across the hall. Oh, Sylvia, it's so lovely to see you. I almost wish I weren't going to Cheltenham.

Sylvia Nonsense, it's your only little holiday. I know how you look forward to it.

Mavis Yes, I do. And I can't very well stay here. We haven't enough beds for all of us.

Sylvia There you are then. It's Cox and Box, I'm afraid. But we'll have a lovely talk when you get back. When does your train go?

Mavis At three o'clock. The cab will be here at any moment and I haven't told you all the things you need to know. The baker calls every day. The butcher on Tuesdays and Thursdays, the fishmonger on Fridays. Mother likes a bath in the morning twice a week. The kitchen boiler takes a bit of lighting—you need to give it a good draught. If you bank it up last thing at night it should stay in . . .

Sylvia Mavis! I have never lit a boiler in my life! Doesn't the maid do it?

Mavis Oh no. We haven't a maid. We're not very well off, you know.

Sylvia (*after a pause*) So you do everything.

Mavis Well . . . yes. There's only the two of us. Mother doesn't consider we need a maid.

Sylvia I see. (*She lifts her chin*) Then we must manage without. I dare say one week won't kill us.

Mavis Don't do any cleaning. I've cleaned through and done all the washing and ironing. Just see to the meals and look after Mother.

Sylvia What if she becomes ill? Where does the doctor live?

Mavis Just across the bridge, next to the church. Mother's doctor is Dr Thorne, but unfortunately he's away at a conference, so in an emergency you must send for his partner, Dr Parry.

Sylvia Doesn't she like Dr Parry?

Mavis Actually she prefers him to Dr Thorne because he's young and handsome and she can flirt with him. Dr Thorne is middle-aged and doesn't mince his words and tells her not to be a tiresome old woman . . . but he's a more experienced doctor. Oh, see she takes her heart pills every evening at bedtime. She makes a fuss about swallowing them but she must do it. Now, what else was there? I'm sure I've forgotten something.

Sylvia Oh do stop worrying, Mavis. We shall be perfectly all right, I promise you.

Mavis Yes. Of course you will. I know *you'll* be all right, Sylvia. Mother is so happy to have you here. I . . . I hope Rose will be all right, too. She's . . . so like me. It's a great pity.

Sylvia Mavis, what on earth do you mean? Mother isn't some sort of gorgon. She's a dear old lady who needs lots of love and we're going to give it to her.

Mavis And it's only for a week. Nothing much can go wrong in a week.

Mrs Bell enters, wearing the shawl, and followed by Rose

Mrs Bell (*plaintively*) Mavis, have you seen my emerald brooch? I want to
try it on my new shawl.

Mavis puts her hand to the brooch she is wearing

Mavis Your emerald ...

Mrs Bell (*amazed and pained*) Mavis, you're wearing it! That's very wrong
of you, to take my brooch without asking. If you wanted to borrow it you
had only to say so.

Mavis But Mother, you gave it me.

Mrs Bell Gave it you? Are you out of your mind? I wouldn't give away
Father's brooch, the last present he ever gave me.

Mavis But you *did*, only this afternoon. You said I was to keep it and wear
it at Cheltenham.

Mrs Bell Now Mavis, I'm ashamed of you, for making up such a story in
front of Sylvia and Rose. I'm afraid your brain is confused. I know you're
at a difficult age, dear, but you mustn't let your day dreams interfere with
reality. Father's brooch is very precious to me, as you should know ...

Mavis fumbles with the brooch and thrusts it into Mrs Bell's hands

Mavis (*in tears*) Here, take it back. I never wanted it anyhow.

Mavis exits, weeping

Mrs Bell Oh dear, now she's crying. I never meant to upset her but,
honestly, to take Father's brooch and pretend that I gave it to her ...

Sylvia I'll go after her. I'm sure it was a misunderstanding.

Sylvia exits

Mrs Bell I don't see how a misunderstanding like *that* could arise.

Rose Well ... perhaps she asked if she could borrow it and you thought she
was talking about something else ... a book perhaps ... and you said
"yes" without realizing.

Mrs Bell Rose, I am seventy-five years old and my heart is faulty but there
is nothing wrong with my hearing. In any case, the scene you have
envisaged is nothing like Mavis's version of the affair. She says that I gave
it to her, which is a downright lie.

Rose Oh dear. And she's leaving soon. You *will* forgive her before she goes,
won't you, Grandma? She's so upset.

Mrs Bell I suppose I shall have to. When you're older, Rose, perhaps you'll
know a bit more about what middle age does to maiden ladies. They can
be very difficult to live with.

Mrs Bell exits

Rose wanders to the small window

Behind her back Ellen comes to the garden window and peers in

*When Rose turns and gasps, she dodges out of sight. Rose goes and opens the
garden door*

Rose What are you doing?

Ellen (*off*) Nothing.

Rose Yes, you were. You were looking in at me.

She drags Ellen in by the wrist

Rose What's your name?

Ellen Ellen. I live next door.

Rose What are you doing, peering in like that, scaring me to death?

Ellen Well, actually I was hoping to catch a glimpse of you. I didn't mean to frighten you. You're Rose, aren't you? Your Grandmother's been talking about you for weeks.

Rose And am I what you expected?

Ellen No, not a bit. She said you'd be beautiful.

Rose And I'm not, am I?

Ellen Not really. What happened to your hair?

Rose I cut if off.

Ellen Weren't you sorry afterwards?

Rose No. I feel wonderfully light-headed.

Ellen Does your grandmother like it?

Rose I don't think so. She hasn't said, but her face spoke volumes!

Ellen (*after a pause*) She *did* give it her, you know.

Rose What?

Ellen Your Gran. She did give the brooch to your Aunt Mavis.

Rose (*staring*) How do you know? Were you there?

Ellen No. I was outside the window, listening.

Rose Do you do a lot of that . . . listening?

Ellen Yes. I know it's wrong of me but . . . I lead a terribly dull life and nobody ever tells me anything and I do so long to know what's going on. What's *really* going on.

Rose You must find out a lot of things that way.

Ellen Yes. But I don't tell anybody—usually.

Rose I think in this case you'd better tell me all you can. I don't approve of eavesdropping you know, but this little mystery needs clearing up. Come and sit on the sofa.

They sit side by side

Ellen Well, Mrs Bell sent for her jewel box and asked for that brooch . . .

Rose You're sure it was the same one?

Ellen It must have been. I heard her say "the emerald brooch" and your aunt said, "Oh no, you can't give away Father's brooch" and the old lady said, "Yes, I can. I've got plenty of others, and you're to wear it at Cheltenham." And she made your aunt give her a kiss. Just after that, your carriage arrived.

Rose But that's incredible. Grandmother can't have *such* a short memory.

Ellen Perhaps she's got softening of the brain. That's what my mother says my father's got.

Rose I expect you mean senile decay. That's what old people get. But I can't believe Grandmother's brain could be going.

Ellen No wonder your aunt looks so miserable always.

Rose Does she?

Ellen It can't be much fun living with somone that's going off her head.

Rose I don't believe she *is*. Either it was a momentary aberration or else . . .

Ellen Or else what?

Rose (*getting up*) Never mind. Who's that, coming up the garden path?

Ellen (*joining her at the window*) Oh, that's Dr Parry. Don't you think he's handsome?

Rose Not bad.

Ellen I think he's wonderful. I keep trying to be ill, but Mother says I'm disgustingly healthy. None of our family ever suffers from anything.

Rose Only softening of the brain.

They giggle

   Dr Parry comes in at the garden door

Dr Parry Oh. Good afternoon. I was looking for Mrs Bell.

Rose She's upstairs, I think. Can I give her a message? I'm her granddaughter.

Dr Parry Oh. How do you do, Miss . . . er. . .

Rose Morley. Rose Morley.

Dr Parry I'm James Parry. (*They shake hands*)

Rose Yes, Ellen told me.

Dr Parry You're just back from Ceylon, I believe.

Rose Yes.

Ellen That's why she's such a funny colour. Is your mother the same?

Rose No, Mother never goes out in the sun without a parasol. In Ceylon they thought *she* was a funny colour.

Dr Parry Is there much illness out there?

Rose There's quite a lot of beri-beri among the poor people. My father reckoned it was due to poor diet. He used to try and get his workers to change their eating habits, but they just wouldn't.

Dr Parry Your father was probably right. I have a friend who went to India to work and he's doing research along the same lines.

Rose Won't you sit down?

Dr Parry I'd like to but I've got to dash off and treat someone in the village. The trouble is, I can't remember who. I shall have to go back and consult my diary. (*He looks at Ellen*) On second thoughts, perhaps I needn't. I've always found Ellen a mine of information. Ellen, who is most likely to be in need of my skills this afternoon?

Ellen (*thinking*) Well . . . Johnny Sykes has the measles.

Dr Parry I saw him this morning. He was quite a sight.

Ellen . . . and Mr Norris got his foot run over by a hay waggon . . .

Dr Parry Yes. I've dealt with him, too.

Ellen It wouldn't be young Mrs Butler, would it?

Dr Parry Hardly. She's not due for another six weeks.

Ellen The Murphy boys raided our orchard last night.

Dr Parry Yes, they may well have a nasty bout of colic but they're keeping quiet about it. Come on, Ellen, don't let me down.

Ellen (*thinking hard*) Mrs Hardy was breathing very heavily in church last Sunday. It's her bronchitis.

Dr Parry It's nothing of the sort. She was fast asleep and snoring. It's no good, Ellen, I shall have to go back and get my diary.

He turns to go

Rose Dr Parry!

He turns back

What was the message for my grandmother?

Dr Parry Oh yes, I forgot. Please tell her that I've left my tools in the porch by the back door and I'll come and cut the grass next Saturday afternoon.

Rose That's very kind. I know she'll be grateful.

Dr Parry exits by the garden door

Ellen Oh! I've just remembered. The post office was closed all morning. Miss Frost must be ill. Dr Parry! Dr Parry!

Ellen runs off after Dr Parry

Rose stands smiling

Mrs Bell enters

Mrs Bell I thought I heard voices.

Rose Yes. Dr Parry was here. He said he'd come and cut the grass for you next Saturday afternoon.

Mrs Bell Ah, good. Did he say anything else?

Rose Not to me. Most of the time he was talking to Ellen.

Mrs Bell That's not surprising. She's a very pretty girl.

Rose Yes, very.

Mrs Bell (*looking at her in exasperation*) Do you *have* to wear those appalling spectacles?

Rose (*mildly*) No, I don't *have* to. But I prefer to see things clearly, rather than just a blur.

Mrs Bell I don't understand it. When I was your age I'd rather have been blind than wear such ugly things.

Rose (*smiling*) Oh, Grandma, I'm sure you wouldn't.

Sylvia enters

How's Aunt Mavis, Mother?

Sylvia I think she's all right again. She's quite composed now.

Mrs Bell What did she say, about the emerald brooch?

Sylvia Absolutely nothing. When I tried to find out the cause of the misunderstanding, she just said, "Please, Sylvia, don't talk about it," and changed the subject.

Mrs Bell No wonder she doesn't want to talk about. She hasn't a leg to stand on.

Sylvia Mother, you won't ...

Mrs Bell All right, I know what you mean. I won't say anything more, just as she's going on holiday. I hate these scenes as much as you do ... but I'm hurt, deeply hurt. And more than that, I'm worried.

Rose Worried, Grandma?

Mrs Bell You wouldn't understand, child. Women of that age have been known to ... go out of their minds.

Sylvia Mavis is all right. She just needs a holiday.

Mrs Bell Well, I can't let her go with bad feeling between us. Sylvia, go up and tell her to be sure and come and kiss me goodbye. Will you do that, dear?

Sylvia (*eagerly*) Of course I will.

Sylvia exits

Mrs Bell sits

Mrs Bell Oh dear, my legs do ache so. I usually get Mavis to rub them for me, with embrocation.

Rose (*willingly*) I'll do it for you, if you like. Where's the stuff?

Mrs Bell Later. Later. After she's gone. (*She picks up the wooden carving*) Now, where shall we put this remarkable piece of carving? On the mantelpiece, I think. Will you put it in the centre for me, Rose?

Rose takes the carving to the mantelpiece

Rose I don't think there's room.

Mrs Bell Nonsense, you must *make* room. Push the other things along. Go on. Further. Further along.

Following her instructions, Rose pushes objects along until the end vase falls off and breaks

Rose Oh! How awful of me! I'm terribly sorry, Grandma! I hope it wasn't valuable. (*She goes down on her knees to pick up the pieces*)

Mrs Bell (*in a fury*) Valuable? It was priceless!

Rose Priceless?

Mrs Bell It was rare Limoges china. It's been in my family for years. An antique collector once offered me a hundred pounds for that vase and I wouldn't part with it. Oh, my vase, my precious Limoges vase! (*She rocks to and fro in distress*)

Mavis enters in outdoor cloak and hat. She sees Rose on her knees, picking up the pieces

Sylvia enters

Mavis Oh dear, had an accident?

Rose (*very contrite*) I'm terribly sorry, Aunt Mavis. I don't know what I can do. Perhaps the pieces could be glued together again ...

Mavis Oh, don't waste tears on that old thing, dear. I'm glad to see the back of it.

Rose But it's valuable.

Mavis Valuable? I got it in a jumble sale for a halfpenny.

Rose (*rising to her feet*) Oh!

Sylvia We'll clear up after Mavis has gone. The cab has arrived.
Mavis (*going to Mrs Bell*) Good-bye, Mother.
Mrs Bell Good-bye, dear. Have a nice time at Cheltenham.

Mrs Bell and Mavis kiss without warmth

Remember me to Bertha.
Mavis I will. Take care of yourself, Mother.
Mrs Bell Don't worry about me, dear. Sylvia and Rose will take good care
of me. Now off you go or you'll miss the train.
Mavis (*kissing Rose*) Good-bye, Rose dear. I hope ... I hope you'll be all
right.
Rose Good-bye, Auntie. Have a lovely holiday.
Sylvia Come on, we'll wave you good-bye. Mother can wave from the
window.

Sylvia and Mavis go out

Rose pauses in the door way and looks challengingly at her grandmother

Rose Grandma. Why did you say that was a valuable vase, when you knew
it was bought at a jumble sale for a halfpenny?
Mrs Bell Because I was fond of it. And I was angry with you for breaking it.
Rose But I was *terribly* upset. You must have known I would be.
Mrs Bell Yes. I meant you to be.
Rose Why?
Mrs Bell To pay you out. For your clumsiness. I can't abide clumsy people.

Rose glares at her

Dear God, child, how plain you are! One can only hope that you have a
nice nature to compensate.
Rose (*deliberately*) I shouldn't rely on that, Grandmother, if I were you.

Rose exits

The Lights fade

CURTAIN

SCENE 2

Saturday morning, a week later

*Rose, wearing an apron, is on her knees cleaning the grate and she has smudges
of black on her face*

The bell of the front door rings

Rose Oh, dear.

She waits, on her knees, listening. The bell rings again. She rises

Hang it, where's Mother gone?

She goes out, leaving the door open, and is heard to open the front door

Arthur (*off*) Good morning. Is your mistress about, young lady?
Rose (*off*) My mistress?
Arthur (*off*) Yes. I was hoping to see Mrs Bell. Is she still alive?
Rose (*off*) Oh yes, she's alive all right.
Arthur (*off*) Good.

Arthur Fox comes into view in the hall, a rather common, self-important man of fifty

I was afraid the good soul might have passed on. And is she at home?

Rose follows Arthur on

Rose That depends what you mean.
Arthur (*coming into the room and looking about him*) I should have thought it was a simple enough question. Is your mistress at home?
Rose Well, yes and no.
Arthur (*staring*) Yes and no?
Rose I mean, yes, she's at home physically but no, she's not at home to visitors. You see, she's not up from bed yet. She never rises till ten o'clock.
Arthur Oh, I see. Of course, I should have thought of that. She's quite an old lady now, isn't she? When I knew her she was a sprightly woman in her middle fifties. That was twenty years ago, of course.
Rose If you'd like to call back, I'm sure she'd be pleased to see you.
Arthur Yes, I'll do that. Will you tell her that Arthur Fox called?
Rose Arthur Fox?
Arthur That's right. I expect she'll remember me. Just say I was in the district and I thought it would be nice to talk over old times.
Rose (*smiling at him*) I expect Mrs Bell would enjoy that.
Arthur I'll be back later this morning if I may.
Rose (*ushering him out*) Very well, sir. Good morning, sir.
Arthur Good morning.

Rose and Arthur go out. Rose returns immediately, smiling

Rose sighs and kneels by the grate to resume work

Sylvia (*off; calling*) Rose! Rose Where are you?
Rose In here, Mother.

Sylvia enters, carrying an unfolded sheet

Sylvia Darling, help me fold this sheet, will you? My arms aren't long enough to keep it off the ground.
Rose (*rising*) My hands are all dirty.
Sylvia Oh, wipe them on your skirt.

Rose does so and they open up the sheet and then fold it

It's only half dry, but I decided to bring it in off the line before it rains.
Rose I thought Aunt Mavis said not to change the sheets.

Sylvia She didn't reckon on Mother spilling her tea all over them. There, that's better. Now I can hang it on the clothes horse in the kitchen.

Rose Is the boiler still lit?

Sylvia Just about, but it's hovering between life and death. If it goes out again I shall scream. How Mavis manages all on her own I don't know. I'm quite exhausted, and you must be run off your legs with fetching and carrying.

Rose I'm all right.

Sylvia You're looking a bit peaky, dear. Are you *sure* you're all right?

Rose I've not been sleeping very well.

Sylvia Haven't you? I have. I'm so tired every night, I'm unconscious before I touch the pillow. But I don't mind, as long as Mavis is getting a rest and Mother's enjoying our company, bless her heart. Wasn't she in her element last night, showing us her old souvenirs and pictures?

Rose She was very good looking, wasn't she?

Sylvia Quite a beauty, I believe—and an outrageous flirt if one can believe all she says. Isn't it a shame that beauty fades and old age gets us in the end.

Rose That's why she wants her family to carry on the tradition. Your beauty must be a great comfort to her.

Sylvia Well, I hope she'll bear it in mind next time I burn the porridge! You were an angel to take the blame.

Rose (*at the small window,* L) Is that the postman at the gate?

Sylvia I hope so. There's Ellen, too. He's giving her something for us.

Rose I bet it's another of Auntie's exciting picture postcards. A view of the Pump Room again, I expect.

Sylvia Oh no, we've had two different views of that already.

Rose D'you think Auntie is taking the waters?

Sylvia As far as I'm concerned, she can keep them. I believe they taste vile.

The front door is heard to open and Ellen appears in the doorway

Ellen (*knocking*) May I come in? Are you busy?

Rose We never stop. But come in anyway.

Ellen I've a postcard for you. (*She gives it to Sylvia*)

Sylvia It's not the Pump Room anyway. The Montpelier Rotunda. (*She turns it over*) "This is a fine regency building, designed partly by Papworth ... only I'm not sure which part! Home on Saturday, half past five. Mavis."

Ellen You'll be glad to see her home again, I expect.

Sylvia You never said a truer word. The responsibility for getting dinner every day is turning me grey. Rose, did we decide on steak and kidney pudding or pie? Not that there's much difference, the way I make it.

A small hand-bell rings off stage

There's Mother's bell. Whatever does she want now?

Sylvia exits

Ellen Your grandmother keeps you on the go, doesn't she?

Rose Yes. Is she as bad with Aunt Mavis?

Ellen I suppose so. It isn't so much that she keeps her busy, but she doesn't seem to *like* her very much, if you know what I mean.

Rose Oh, I know what you mean all right.

Ellen She likes your mother, though. I can tell.

Rose You notice a not, don't you, Ellen?

Ellen I'm sorry, it's nosey of me, isn't it? But if you knew how dull my life is ...

She sits rather heavily on Gran's chair. It tilts sideways and she nearly falls off. She gives a little scream

Oh! Something gave!

Rose What d'you mean, something gave?

Ellen I don't know. It tipped right over.

They turn the seat upside down and examine it

Rose Look! The castor has come right off.

Ellen It's a bit dangerous for your grandmother to sit on. It gave me an awful fright.

Rose I reckon I could mend it. I've often helped my father with bits of carpentry. Ellen, can you go to the back porch for me? There's a cupboard full of tools. Bring me the tool box.

Ellen hurries out, bumping into Dr Parry who is entering with a small bottle of medicine

Rose is on her knees by the upturned chair

Dr Parry Hello, something wrong? Anything I can do?

Rose Yes, if you can wield a hammer.

Dr Parry Of course I can wield a hammer. How do you suppose I put my patients to sleep? (*He kneels down by the chair*) What's wrong with the invalid, Nurse?

Rose It's gone lame in one leg.

Dr Parry Hm. Tut tut. (*He looks it over carefully*) We shall have to perform an operation. It might require amputation. Are your nerves strong enough to be present while it takes place, Nurse?

Rose I shall try not to faint, Doctor.

Dr Parry Good. A woman of strong character. Where are my surgical instruments?

Ellen hurries in with tools

Rose Just coming, Doctor.

Dr Parry (*turning up his sleeves*) Splendid. Stand by, Ladies. We'll have this set right before you can say ninety-nine. Hold the patient's hand ... er ... foot, I should say.

Ellen steadies the chair by its leg

Rose Every time you call we find a job for you. I feel ashamed.

Dr Parry Please don't. It's nice to be needed.

Rose On Monday it was unblocking the sink. On Wednesday it was sharpening the scissors. On Friday it was . . . (*She fails to remember*)

Ellen Picking plums up the ladder.

Rose And now this.

Dr Parry Yes. Disgraceful. I don't know why I keep coming.

Ellen Why *do* you keep on coming?

Dr Parry To keep an eye on Mrs Bell, of course. Dr Thorne told me to give her every care during his absence.

Sylvia enters with a warming-pan

Sylvia Rose, Mother wants this warming-pan cleaned. Have you got time?

Rose I'll make time.

She takes the warming pan and holds it like a ukelele

Sylvia Hello, Doctor. Don't get up, I can see you're busy. (*She looks at Rose and has a sudden fit of laughter*) Rose, your face is all smutty and you look just like a nigger minstrel about to burst into song.

Rose strikes an attitude and strums her "ukelele"

Rose If you had a banjo we could do the party piece that we used to do every Christmas.

Sylvia looks round and picks up a clean shovel

Sylvia This'll do! Can you remember the steps?

Rose I think so.

They sing "The Camptown Races" in minstrel fashion, strumming their "banjo" strutting up and down, sitting on the sofa with legs crossed at the knee, kicking up their legs and showing frilly petticoats—a very lively performance. Dr Parry punctuates each verse with a flourish of hammer on wood

In the middle of the fun Mrs Bell comes in and watches with a smile

When it is over Mrs Bell, Ellen and Dr Parry clap warmly. Sylvia and Rose curtsy

Mrs Bell Lovely! Lovely! As good as a visit to a seaside concert. Oh, it does my heart good to hear singing and laughter around me. Good morning, Dr Parry. Whatever are you doing to my chair?

Dr Parry Just making it quite safe. The legs were a bit wobbly.

Mrs Bell So are mine but I doubt if a hammer and nails would do them much good.

Rose I'd better go and get the Brasso.

Mrs Bell Yes, and while you're in the kitchen, dear, for goodness sake wash your face.

Rose (*pausing in the doorway*) Oh, I nearly forgot. A gentleman called.

Sylvia A gentleman? When?

Rose This morning. I told him to call back later. He said his name was
Arthur Fox.

Rose exits

*At the name "Arthur Fox", both Sylvia and her mother freeze. Sylvia is
startled but her mother is appalled. They look at each other and then look at
Ellen and Dr Parry who are absorbed in their repair work*

Sylvia (*lowering her voice*) It can't be the same man, can it?

Mrs Bell Of course it's the same man. What can we do?

Sylvia Well, we can hardly turn him away.

Mrs Bell I don't want to see him, Sylvia. I shall say I'm ill.

Sylvia No, please don't leave me to deal with him on my own. What a pity
Mavis isn't here.

Mrs Bell On the contrary, it would be far worse if Mavis were here.

Sylvia I suppose so. I wonder if he's changed. It must be twenty years. I
wonder if he still says "Ee, ba gum!" I shall giggle if he does. Oh
goodness, I'll never get the beans done in time for dinner. Ellen, can you
slice beans?

Ellen Yes, I think so.

Sylvia Good. Then come with me. Everyone who sets foot in this house gets
pressed into service.

Sylvia exits followed by a rather unwilling Ellen

Mrs Bell That's true. I hope you aren't neglecting your patients, young
man. (*Sweetly*) I'm glad to have my chair mended, but I don't want Dr
Thorne to give you a rap on the knuckles when he gets back.

Dr Parry Don't worry, Mrs Bell. I've dealt with all the urgent cases. This
one comes under the heading of "casualty". (*He rises*) It's done now. I'll
just test it, to see if it'll bear my weight. (*He sits for a moment*) Yes, I think
you'll be safe on that.

He rises and Mrs Bell takes his place

Mrs Bell Good. My favourite, comfy old chair. I *always* sit in this one, you
know. Nobody else is allowed on it. I'm very much obliged to you, Dr
Parry.

Dr Parry (*turning down his sleeves*) I really came round to bring you some
new medicine. (*He shows her the bottle*)

Mrs Bell Oh indeed? What is it for?

Dr Parry For your heart. It's the same as the pills really, but easier to
swallow. I know you have difficulty swallowing pills.

Mrs Bell Does it taste nasty?

Dr Parry Faintly unpleasant. Nothing more. A toffee afterwards might be a
good idea.

Mrs Bell A toffee would be a splendid idea, especially under doctor's
orders.

Dr Parry picks up the hammer and nails

Dr Parry I'll take these out to the back porch as I go. Oh, by the way I had

hoped to cut your grass this afternoon but it's coming on to rain. Shall I
leave my tools a bit longer, till the weather picks up?

Mrs Bell Yes, of course. They won't be in anyone's way.

Dr Parry Good day then, Mrs Bell.

Mrs Bell Good day, Dr Parry. Thank you for the medicine.

Dr Parry Don't forget, you take it *instead* of the pills, not as *well*.

Mrs Bell I'll remember.

Dr Parry exits

Mrs Bell sits back in her chair with a pleased smile

Rose enters, with a clean face, and carrying the Brasso

Mrs Bell You're too late.

Rose Too late? What for?

Mrs Bell Dr Parry has gone. All the time he was here you had a grubby,
repulsive face. Now you look reasonably clean and tidy, he has gone.

Rose (*philosophically*) Oh, never mind.

Mrs Bell Never mind? I do mind and so should you. If you cared a bit more
about appearances you wouldn't have made such an exhibition of
yourself just now.

Rose (*staring*) An exhibition of myself?

Mrs Bell A disgraceful exhibition, carrying on like any vulgar chorus girl,
kicking up your legs, prancing about singing common American songs—
the sort of spectacle one might see on the end of the pier, not in one's own
drawing-room.

Rose But you clapped. You said it was lovely.

Mrs Bell I had no wish to let you down in front of your visitors.

Rose You said you loved to hear singing. Only last night you said *you* used
to sing at parties.

Mrs Bell When I sang, I sang "The Last Rose of Summer". I stood
demurely by the piano with my fan in my hand. I kept both feet on the
ground. I did not cavort around the room perspiring in front of
gentlemen. I was *ashamed* of you.

Rose What about Mother? Were you ashamed of her, too?

Mrs Bell Your mother is different. Whatever she does, she carries it off with
grace and charm. In any case, your mother has no need to capture a beau.

Rose Capture a beau! Honestly, Grandma, that's a silly expression.

Mrs Bell Don't you tell me what's silly, my girl. You ought to take a leaf
out of Ellen's book. She wears perfume.

Rose Yes. I've noticed.

Mrs Bell And instead of throwing herself into unladylike postures, she knelt
very close to the doctor and let her proximity cast a spell. It's amazing
what perfume and proximity can do to a man.

Rose That's disgusting. (*She polishes the warming-pan*)

Mrs Bell (*incensed*) You dare to call me disgusting?

Rose What I find disgusting is the whole idea of trying to trap a man, by fair
means or foul. You talk as if a woman has no purpose in life but to get
married.

Mrs Bell What other choice is there for her? Marriage is the only way a woman can find security and a home of her own. Scoff at your peril, young woman. You have few enough natural graces. You would do well to learn a few while you're young or you'll end up an old maid, like your Aunt Mavis.

Rose I'm not ashamed of being like Aunt Mavis. She's sweet and kind—and where would you be without her?

Mrs Bell Oh, I admit all that. She's a useful person to have around, and what's more, she doesn't answer back like you do. I don't know what I've done to deserve such an impolite grand-daughter.

Rose Grandma, I started off as polite as can be. I *am* polite by nature. But ever since I set foot in this house you have constantly tried to humiliate me, starting with the affair of the jumble sale vase, and my politeness has been strained beyond endurance. You never do it in front of Mother, only when we're alone.

Mrs Bell I don't know what you mean.

Rose If I bring you flowers, you develop hay fever. If I fill your hot water bottle, it scalds your feet. If I read to you, my voice jars on your ears. When I play the piano you say what a pity that I'm so heavy-handed. One day there was a wasp annoying you, so I killed it and was blamed for hurting one of God's dumb creatures. One day you saw a funeral going down the street and sent me out to find out whose it was. On my return you complained bitterly about my morbid obsession with death. I can do nothing right. I've had biting comments on my hair, my complexion, my figure, my voice, my cooking and my conversation. And yesterday, you excelled yourself. Yesterday, you said you were ill and I was sent running for the doctor. But when he came you were up and about with nothing the matter with you, and you told Dr Parry—you actually told Dr Parry—that I had made the whole thing up as an excuse to get his attention! And then, when I blushed, do you know what you said? "What a pity you don't blush prettily like Ellen does."

Mrs Bell Ah! So you do care what the doctor thinks of you!

Rose I'm sick and tired of being compared with Ellen. I have very little doubt that Aunt Mavis has spent all *her* life being compared with *Mother*. But I want you to understand, Grandmother, that I'm not like Aunt Mavis as much as it may seem. You're not going to break my spirit and I very much doubt if you can make me cry.

Mrs Bell We shall see. Have you finished this outrageous outburst?

Rose It will do, for the time being. I don't want Mother to come in and find us quarrelling.

She rubs vigorously at the warming pan. Mrs Bell stares at her, breathing heavily for a while

Mrs Bell There's not much point in making that thing shine. You can hardly want to see your face in it!

She looks out of the small window L *and exclaims in annoyance*

Oh, drat it, there's someone coming to call.

Rose (*looking over her shoulder*) That's Mr Fox. I told you he was coming back this morning.

Mrs Bell I don't want to see him. You should have said I was dead.

Rose Who is he and why don't you want to see him?

Mrs Bell If you *must* know, he was your Aunt Mavis's only admirer and she let him slip through her fingers.

The door bell rings

Rose Am I to let him in or direct him to the graveyard?

Sylvia enters carrying a tray with a half-full wine decanter and wine glasses

Sylvia Let him in, Rose, will you? My hands are full.

Rose exits

(*Putting the tray on the sideboard*) I brought some wine, Mother. Is that all right?

Mrs Bell Well, only one glass and get rid of him as soon as possible. He's got no right coming here and raking up the past.

Rose (*off*) Yes, Mr Fox, she's up now. I told her you were coming. Shall I take your hat?

Arthur (*off*) Thank you, my dear.

Arthur enters followed by Rose

Mrs Bell! Do you remember me? Arthur Fox?

Mrs Bell (*graciously allowing him to take her hand*) Of course I remember you, Mr Fox. This is a great surprise.

Arthur (*turning to Sylvia*) And Miss Bell. There's no mistaking you, even after twenty years.

Sylvia Mrs Morley now, Mr Fox.

Arthur You used to call me Arthur in those days, do you remember?

Sylvia Of course I do ... Arthur ... and this is my daughter, Rose.

Arthur Your daughter? Why goodness me, Miss Rose, I do apologize. I took you for the maid.

Rose (*smiling*) I know you did.

Mrs Bell Our maid is, unfortunately, indisposed.

Rose She's been indisposed for a long time.

Arthur I'm sorry to hear it.

Sylvia Won't you sit down, Arthur?

Arthur Thank you. And where is Miss Mavis? Left home years ago, I expect.

Mrs Bell (*before anyone can answer*) Yes. A long time ago.

Sylvia and Rose stare at her

Arthur Where is she living now?

Mrs Bell Cheltenham.

Arthur Oh. That's a pity. I'm so sorry to have missed her.

Sylvia Er ... where are *you* living now, Arthur?

Arthur Bradford, my home town. Doing very nicely, too. Took on my father's woollen business when he died. Married a Bradford girl and had two lads.

Mrs Bell And is your wife here too, Mr Fox?

Arthur (*looking grave*) Nay, I'm afraid not. She passed on a year ago with a nasty bout of influenza. I'm a lonely widower, now.

Sylvia I'm so sorry. And what are you doing in these parts after so long? (*She goes to the sideboard to pour wine*)

Arthur It's a business trip, really. Trying to get a few new contacts in the retail trade ... and finding myself in your vicinity I couldn't resist a chance to look you up.

Sylvia Will you take a glass of wine with us?

Arthur It'll be a great pleasure. By gum, Sylvia, how this brings back the old days. Taking wine in the parlour after church on Sundays. You had a pink bonnet, I remember, with roses on it.

Sylvia (*handing wine to everyone*) I remember.

Arthur And Mavis had a lavender coloured dress that suited her a marvel. Ee, I'll always remember how she looked in that lavender dress.

Mrs Bell Quite the wrong colour for a girl of that complexion.

Arthur It went very nicely with her hair. She had pretty hair. I suppose she's grey now.

Mrs Bell Yes. Very.

Arthur And I'm going bald. It's sad, isn't it, how quickly life passes. One minute you're young and handsome ... the next minute you're getting measured for your coffin.

Rose Please don't talk of death in front of Grandmother, Mr Fox. She finds it morbid and depressing, don't you, Grandma?

Mrs Bell (*with a laugh*) Nonsense, Rose. I'm not such a sensitive plant and death doesn't frighten me. I realize my heart is failing and I know that the old man with the scythe will be coming to get me one day ... but I must admit (*roguishly*) I'd go a lot more willingly if a *young* man came for me.

Arthur (*laughing*) Yes, Mrs Bell, you always got on well with the young men. (*He turns to Rose*) It was most noticeable, Miss Rose, whenever there was a party, the men were either gathered round your mother or your grandmother. Still, I didn't mind. It left me more chance to talk to your aunt Mavis. I was ... well ... a bit gone on Mavis, I must admit. Had all sorts of silly, romantic dreams. It came as a bit of a shock to know she was already spoken for.

Sylvia Spoken for?

Arthur Engaged. Of course, as soon as I knew *that*, I gave up coming. Felt as miserable as sin for a long time. But I got over it. You have to, don't you? I hope she's happy in her marriage.

Sylvia But ... Mavis isn't married.

Mrs Bell has a sudden fit of coughing and choking. She struggles to her feet and Sylvia helps her out of the room

Arthur (*rising*) Oh dear, poor old lady. What a nasty little turn.

Rose I shouldn't worry, Mr Fox. She'll get over it. Can I give you some more wine?

Arthur Er ... no, thanks. (*Pause*). Did I hear Sylvia say that her sister *isn't* married?

Rose Yes. Aunt Mavis, never married.

Arthur She broke off this engagement?

Rose What engagement?

Arthur To the other fellow.

Rose Mr Fox, who told you that Aunt Mavis was engaged?

Arthur Her mother did. She took me on one side one day—out there in the garden—and said she was worried because I was getting too fond of Mavis and she thought I ought to know I was wasting my time. She was most kind and sympathetic.

Rose (*bitterly*) I bet she was—the old bitch.

Arthur (*startled*) I beg your pardon?

Rose You never thought to ask Mavis if it was true, did you?

Arthur Well, no. I was a bit cut up, you see. All I wanted was to get away on my own. I felt people were laughing at me.

Rose Mr Fox, you have been the victim of such a cruel trick, I can hardly bear to tell you. My grandmother lied to you. Aunt Mavis was never engaged.

Arthur Never engaged? How can you be so sure?

Rose Only ten minutes ago Grandma said that you were Aunt Mavis's only admirer, and she'd let you slip through her fingers!

Arthur Oh, I think you must be mistaken. Her own mother wouldn't lie about a thing like that.

Rose Wouldn't she just! Can't you see, she didn't want to lose Aunt Mavis—gentle, patient, uncomplaining Aunt Mavis who would wait on her for the rest of her days.

Arthur But that's terrible! It could have ruined her life.

Rose She never married. She never left home.

Arthur Where is she now?

Rose Having her annual week's holiday—at Cheltenham. That's why we're here, to look after Grandma.

Arthur I went through a pretty desperate time, you know, I was so upset. I took to drinking. For nearly a year I was no better than a sot. Then I saw where I was heading and made an effort to get back my self-respect. But poor Mavis ... has she been unhappy?

Rose A week ago I'd have said, I don't know. But I've lived here for a week with Grandma and believe me, I know now. *Yes*, is the answer. Deeply unhappy.

Arthur By gum, if this is true, I won't forgive her in a hurry. Your grandmother hasn't heard the end of this!

He strides out. The back door bangs

Rose stands lost in thought

The Lights fade

CURTAIN

That afternoon, about five o'clock. It is raining heavily outside and there is a rumble of thunder

The room is rather dark, but there is a fire glowing in the hearth. Mrs Bell is sitting alone by the fire

Sylvia enters

Sylvia Why, Mother, you're all alone. I thought Rose was with you.
Mrs Bell She's gone down to the baker's.
Sylvia In this rain?
Mrs Bell I tried to dissuade her but she'd got this idea that she'd like toasted tea cakes for tea and nothing would stop her. She's a very headstrong girl, Sylvia.
Sylvia (*smiling*) Determined, certainly.
Mrs Bell She could catch a chill with getting wet through.
Sylvia Not she. Rose is very tough.
Mrs Bell Most girls would be afraid to be out in a thunder storm.
Sylvia It takes a lot to frighten *that* girl. Sometimes she amazes me, she's so brave, and so . . . well . . . strong minded. Do you know, last year she saw a native whipping his dog and she grabbed the whip out of his hand and whipped him half way up the street.
Mrs Bell Good gracious me!
Sylvia And the strange thing was, she had tears running down her cheeks all the while she was whipping him.
Mrs Bell She *can* cry then?
Sylvia Oh yes, but it's very rare. Not like me. I cry at the least little thing. I nearly cried just now when I discovered that the kitchen boiler had gone out.
Mrs Bell Oh, leave it, dear. Mavis will be home tonight. She'll re-light it for us. Meanwhile we have this nice warm fire to cheer us. Let's draw the curtains and shut out the storm.
Sylvia Draw the curtains? At five o'clock on a September afternoon?
Mrs Bell Yes, draw them. It's so dismal outside that I want to forget it.

Sylvia draws the curtains

That's right. We can sit by the fire and pretend it's Christmas.
Sylvia Shall I light the lamps?
Mrs Bell Light just one. Mustn't be extravagant. (*She sighs*) I don't feel at all well, dear. My heart is acting very strangely.
Sylvia (*with sympathy*) Is it? Oh dear. I expect that choking fit upset you this morning.
Mrs Bell That and the shock of seeing Arthur Fox again. I never liked him when he was younger and twenty years haven't improved him. Common, self-important little man.
Sylvia I felt rather sorry for him. (*She lights the lamp*)
Mrs Bell (*warily*) Sorry for him?

Sylvia Yes. When he was recalling how he had been so fond of Mavis. I know it was ages ago, but it was awfully sad. I wonder why she told him she was engaged?

Mrs Bell Is that what he said? That Mavis told him she was engaged?

Sylvia I think so, didn't he?

Mrs Bell I don't know. I was too busy choking.

Sylvia Silly girl. Perhaps she had some quaint idea that it wasn't proper to seem too eager . . . that he'd want her more if he thought he had a rival . . . just a foolish fib to rouse him to jealousy.

Mrs Bell Huh! Only pretty girls can play tricks like that and get away with it. Mavis should have had more sense. I often wondered what went wrong and she would never tell me. Still, at least it saved me the embarrassment of having Arthur Fox for a son-in-law.

The front door opens

Sylvia That sounds like Rose.

Rose enters in black cloak, hood thrown back, holding a bag of buns

Oh, how wet you are! Why ever did you go out in such awful weather?

Rose I didn't mind the rain. I was feeling like a bit of fresh air so when Grandma said she fancied toasted tea cakes I was happy to go and get them. Here they are, Gran, and here's your purse.

Mrs Bell examines the buns and purse and secretly extracts half a crown

Sylvia Now take off that wet cloak at once, and your stockings too. The boiler's gone out so I don't know where we'll dry them.

Mrs Bell Bring the clothes horse in here. They can dry by the fire. And fetch my medicine, too, dear.

Sylvia exits with the cloak

Rose sits on the sofa and peels off her thick white stockings

How much were the tea cakes?

Rose Threepence.

Mrs Bell In that case, you've got the wrong change.

Rose I can't have. I gave her sixpence and she gave me back three pennies.

Mrs Bell There's half a crown missing.

Rose I'm sure there isn't.

Mrs Bell I must believe the evidence of my own eyes. There were two half crowns here when you set off. Now there's only one.

Rose That's not true.

Mrs Bell Are you calling me a liar?

Rose (*holding back her anger*) I am saying that you are mistaken.

Mrs Bell Do you admit that you had two half crowns when you set out?

Rose Yes.

Mrs Bell (*holding out the purse*) Are they still there?

Rose hops over on one stockinged foot and looks into purse

Well?

Rose One of them has gone.

Mrs Bell Precisely. What did you do with it?

Rose Nothing. If you're trying to suggest that I'm a thief ...

Mrs Bell What else can I think?

Rose There's an obvious alternative.

Mrs Bell What?

Rose That you took it out yourself, just now, and pushed it down the side of the chair.

Mrs Bell Oh! The audacity of it! Can nothing shame you?

Rose There are quite a lot of things could shame me. One of them would be to let you get away with another of your malicious tricks.

Mrs Bell Malicious tricks? I've a good mind to tell your mother about this.

Rose You won't, you know. She's the one person you have any real affection for.

Mrs Bell I do love Sylvia, and I think it's time she knew what was going on.

Rose Well, all right, Grandma, you tell her and we'll see which one of us she believes.

Sylvia enters with a clothes horse, which is already draped with sheets, and also carrying a small bottle of medicine and spoon

Sylvia Here's your medicine, Mother. And the spoon.

She hands the bottle and spoon to Mrs Bell, then turns her back to set up the clothes horse upstage centre, screening the bottom of the door, and drapes the cloak over one corner. Rose brings her wet stockings and spreads them over the sheets, also with her back to Mrs Bell

Your hands are trembling, dear. Are you sure you aren't chilled?

Rose I'm all right, Mother.

Mrs Bell looks round at them, then pulls off her shawl, lays it in the hearth and pours all her medicine over it

Mrs Bell Oh!

They turn

Oh dear, look what I've done!

Sylvia What have you ... ?

Mrs Bell I've upset my medicine, all over my nice new shawl!

Rose Oh, no!

She runs and kneels by the hearth

Sylvia Oh Mother, Rose's beautiful shawl!

Mrs Bell What a horrid, sticky mess! I don't know how I could be so clumsy.

Sylvia I expect it will wash out.

Mrs Bell I'm sure I hope so. I wouldn't like it to be stained that nasty colour for the rest of its days.

Rose's shoulders are shaking

Sylvia Rose, darling, don't cry. Gran couldn't help it.

Mrs Bell Don't tell me Rose is *crying*.

Sylvia Gran's hands are very shaky. Try to understand, darling.

Mrs Bell I never thought I could make Rose *cry*.

Rose (*through her tears*) You did it on purpose!

Sylvia Darling! That's silly. Gran wouldn't. What an idea!

Rose She would! She did! You just don't know, Mama, you just don't know! My beautiful shawl! I worked on it for nearly a year. It was a token of love for the grandmother I'd never seen ... and she did this to it, to spite me.

Sylvia Rose, that's ridiculous. Why should she?

Rose (*weeping*) Because she hates me. She despises me because I'm plain and she hates me because I see through her. All the sweetness and gentle smiles are just reserved for you, her favourite. It's a different story for me and Aunt Mavis.

Sylvia Rose! I will not listen to such terrible things, no matter how upset you are. Leave the room at once!

Rose I'm going, I'm going! But you just ask her, who told Arthur Fox that Aunt Mavis was engaged! Who took him out in the garden and warned him off? Who ruined Auntie's one chance of getting away from her? Go on, ask her!

She rushes out, crying

Sylvia (*quietly*) Mother, is this true?

Mrs Bell Is what true?

Sylvia That you sent Arthur Fox away. That you lied to him.

Mrs Bell Of course not.

Sylvia Rose says you did.

Mrs Bell And you'd believe the word of a hysterical child?

Sylvia Rose isn't a child and she's not hysterical. What's more, she was left alone with Arthur when you had that very convenient choking fit.

Mrs Bell Convenient! (*She begins to show signs of heart trouble*)

Sylvia You dreaded Arthur coming back, didn't you? Mother, tell me. I must know the truth.

Mrs Bell It was for her own good. He was a dreadful common man. He'd never have made her happy. (*She pants and clutches her throat. She is not pretending*)

Sylvia Mother, what's wrong?

Mrs Bell My medicine, quick!

Sylvia You've poured it all away.

Mrs Bell My pills then. In my bedroom.

Sylvia (*going*) I'll get them.

Mrs Bell (*with difficulty*) Take the lamp or you'll never see them. I pushed them right to the back of the cupboard.

Sylvia (*taking the lamp*) Keep perfectly still. Don't try to move.

Sylvia exits

Mrs Bell sits panting in the darkened room, lit only by the glow of the fire. She is obviously ill and frightened. The door is open but we cannot see who enters because the open clothes horse screens our view

Mrs Bell It was for your own good, Mavis. It was for your own good. Why aren't you here when I want you, girl? Why do you go gadding off to Cheltenham and leave me? This is where you belong ... always ... for the rest of your days. Mavis! I want you! (*She struggles to her feet. The missing half crown falls to the floor*) (*With a gasp*) What's that? The half-crown? Oh, wherever did it go? (*She bends down to hunt for it, but in vain. After a while she gives up, sobbing, and again collapses in her chair with her eyes shut*)

Silently the clothes horse moves forward until it is alongside the old lady. The cloak and one white stocking are pulled down from behind. The sheets still hide the interior from view

Mrs Bell opens her eyes and blinks at the clothes horse

Somebody moved the clothes horse. Why can't they leave things alone? Oh I do feel peculiar. I could die here, all alone, and nobody would care. I don't want to die all alone. When my mother died, the whole family was gathered at her bedside, crying and praying. That's the way I'd like to go. I told them I wasn't afraid of death. I made it all seem like a joke. I said, I shouldn't mind as long as they sent a *young* man for me. That made them laugh.

In the red glow of the fire, a black hooded figure rises from behind the clothes horse. It has a blank white face and it carries a scythe over one shoulder. Leaning towards the old lady it gives a long sigh. She utters a piercing scream and falls to the floor unconscious

The Lights fade

CURTAIN

ACT II

The same day, about six-thirty. The curtains are still closed and two lamps are lit

Sylvia, Rose and Ellen are seated in silence. They look tense and anxious. The clothes horse, with cloak and one white stocking, is against the rear wall. Ellen's black toy cat is on the sofa, half hidden and ignored. Rose is not wearing her spectacles

Mavis enters, followed by Dr Parry

Sylvia and Rose jump up anxiously

Mavis (*going to Sylvia*) Mother is alive.

They all relax a little

Dr Parry Her heart is in a very bad way, I'm afraid. She seems to have had a very nasty attack. I suspect it was caused by undue excitement. Did she not take her medicine?

Sylvia No. It got spilled.

Dr Parry All of it?

Sylvia Yes. I went to get her pills. When I came back she was unconscious.

Rose (*to Mavis*) Come and sit down, Auntie. You look so tired.

Mavis Thank you, dear. I'm not tired. It's the shock.

Dr Parry It's most unfortunate, Miss Bell, coming home to this after your week's holiday. I gather you were not in the house when it happened?

Mavis No. I arrived just after they had sent for you. I might have got here earlier, I suppose, if I'd come by cab, but I couldn't find one so I walked up. It had stopped raining by then, luckily.

Dr Parry Tell me, Mrs Morley, had she been exerting herself?

Sylvia (*uncomfortably*) No, not at all. She was sitting by the fire, looking forward to toasted tea cakes. But she did say her heart was funny. That's why I went to get her pills.

Mavis You left her sitting in the dark?

Sylvia Yes. She'd asked me to draw the curtains and shut out the storm. She had the firelight. She liked it. She said it was like Christmas.

Mavis Firelight can cast strange shadows.

Rose What d'you mean, Auntie?

Mavis Mother had a nasty fright. She says she saw Death.

Dr Parry Death?

Mavis Yes. I asked her what she meant but I couldn't get a very clear answer. She believed she saw an old man with a scythe.

Dr Parry Where?

Mavis Here in this room.

Rose She was dreaming. We'd been talking about Death coming with his scythe, do you remember? When Arthur Fox was here.

Mavis (*surprised*) Arthur Fox was here?

Sylvia Yes. This morning, Mavis. Such a surprise. He's down here on a business trip and called in to see us. He was very disappointed at missing you.

Mavis How strange, after all these years. Do you think his visit upset Mother?

Sylvia Oh no. Why should it? He only stayed about a quarter of an hour.

Mavis And you talked about death?

Rose It was . . . a sort of joke. Grandmother said she knew that the old man with a scythe would come for her one day, but she'd sooner they sent a *young* man.

Mavis Oh yes. I've heard her make that joke before. I think I can see how it happened. She's half asleep, she vaguely recalls the conversation, she wakes up and sees grotesque shadows cast by the firelight . . .

Ellen No.

Dr Parry What do you mean, no?

Ellen It wasn't like that at all.

Dr Parry How do you know?

Ellen I was looking through the window.

Mavis You were peering in at our window, in the middle of a thunder storm? I don't believe it.

Ellen The rain was over by then, very nearly.

Mavis Does your mother know how many hours you spend snooping around other folks' houses . . . ?

Dr Parry Miss Bell—please—I want to know what Ellen saw.

Sylvia She can't have seen anything. I'd drawn the curtains.

Ellen Not quite; there was a crack.

Rose And what did you see, Ellen?

Ellen (*round-eyed*) I saw a black hooded figure, with a scythe in its hand. I did, I tell you. It sort of loomed over Mrs Bell and she screamed with terror. I nearly screamed too. It was horrible.

Rose (*grinning*) You're making it up, Ellen. Stop pulling our legs.

Ellen I'm not, I tell you. I saw it and so did the old lady.

Dr Parry And did you see the face of this apparition?

Ellen (*sombrely*) Yes.

Expectant pause

Mavis Well? Whose face was it?

Ellen I don't know. It wasn't human.

Mavis Oh, don't encourage the girl. She's making it up.

Ellen (*getting more excited*) I swear I'm not. It was white and sort of blank without any eyes. It was ... just *dead*. (*She hides her face and shudders*) I shall never forget it as long as I live!

Rose goes to her and shakes her

Rose Ellen, stop it at once! You're just trying to frighten us and it's not very nice of you.

Dr Parry Miss Rose, just a minute.

He takes Ellen's hands and looks into her face

The girl is obviously upset. Her hands are cold and she's trembling. I don't think she's lying.

Mavis Doctor, you're surely not suggesting that she saw the figure of Death in this room?

Dr Parry No, but she may have seen someone dressed up.

Mavis Dressed up?

Dr Parry Yes. It occurs to me that there *is* a scythe in this house. I left one in the back porch, ready to cut the long grass. And I believe there's a black cloak on the clothes horse.

Sylvia (*going to it*) Yes, but it hasn't been touched. It's exactly how I left it, after Rose had been shopping.

Mavis Dr Parry, why don't you go and see if the scythe is where you left it?

Dr Parry Yes, I will.

Dr Parry exits

There is a short pause

Sylvia Ellen, why were you peering in at our window just then?

Ellen Why?

Sylvia Yes. It seems an odd thing to do.

Ellen I was looking for Rose. I wanted to give her something. A present.

Rose A present for me?

Ellen Yes. I hadn't said good-bye properly, you see. So I thought I'd come round and give you this. It's some notepaper and envelopes. (*She takes a small packet from her pocket and hands it to Rose*)

Rose Oh, Ellen, how kind of you. Thank you very much.

Ellen I was hoping you might write to me.

Rose Of course I will.

Ellen Life will be so dull after you've gone. If I got a letter from you now and again, it would be something to look forward to.

Rose I will write, Ellen, I promise.

Sylvia Rose, you're not wearing your glasses.

Rose No. I think I've left them upstairs.

Ellen You look so much nicer without them.

Dr Parry enters

Mavis Is the scythe still there?

Dr Parry Yes, but it's now on the left of the door and I'm sure I put it on the right. And that's not all. I found this crumpled white stocking lying beside it.

Rose It looks like one of mine.

Dr Parry Miss Bell, may I put on the cloak a moment? And Mrs Morley, will you blow out the lamps?

Sylvia does so. Dr Parry retires to the rear, turns his back and puts on first the cloak, then the stocking over his head and then the hood. While he is doing this the conversation continues

Mavis Goodness, it's just like a winter evening!

Sylvia Yes. I remember as a child I used to hate that hour before the lamps were lit. In the firelight my shadow always seemed about ten feet tall. And all the ghost stories I'd ever read seemed suddenly . . . quite believable.

Dr Parry turns round and comes forward. At the sight of his blank face they exclaim in horror

Ellen That's it! That's what I saw!

Mavis It's dreadful. No wonder Mother's heart couldn't stand the shock.

Sylvia Mine turned right over.

Rose Dr Parry, for goodness sake, take those things off at once, unless you want a trio of hysterical females to deal with. And let's have some daylight to cheer us.

She draws back the curtains and the room is filled with evening sunshine

The storm is over and it's going to be a beautiful evening.

Dr Parry lays the cloak and stocking over the clothes horse

Dr Parry So, Ellen, you're quite certain that's what you saw?

Ellen Positive. And he had the scythe too. That made it worse.

Dr Parry That means that someone deliberately tried to frighten the old lady to death—and very nearly succeeded.

Mavis That's not a very comfortable thought, Doctor.

Dr Parry I would say it's an appalling thought. If they had succeeded, and Ellen had not chanced to be peering through the window, no-one could have known she hadn't died a natural death.

Ellen That would be murder!

Sylvia Oh, no!

Dr Parry What would *you* call it, Mrs Morley?

Rose I'm sure that, whoever it was never intended to *kill* Grandma—just to frighten her.

Dr Parry This puts me in a very difficult position. If she had died, I'd have been duty bound to report it to the police.

Mavis Oh!

Dr Parry The fact that she survived doesn't wipe the slate clean. At the risk of upsetting you all over again, I feel I'd like to ask a lot more questions.

Mavis Conduct an enquiry, you mean?

Dr Parry Well—very informally. As a friend of the family.

Rose Is it that or the police?

Dr Parry I'm afraid so.

Mavis But no crime has been committed. I don't think I *want* you questioning my family.

Ellen Are you afraid of what he'd find out, Miss Bell?

Dr Parry Keep quiet, Ellen. I can't force these ladies to go through with it if they are unwilling. Are you unwilling, Miss Bell?

Mavis For myself, no.

Dr Parry Mrs Morley?

Sylvia (*hesitating*) Oh dear. This is so upsetting. But I suppose it would be ... better to know the truth. (*She looks nervously at Rose*) Don't you think so, Rose?

Rose (*having looked round at everyone, making up her mind*) Yes. You go ahead, Dr Parry. I may have to admit to a few things I'm ashamed of, but confession is good for the soul.

Dr Parry (*smiling at her*) I felt sure I could count on your co-operation.

Sylvia Won't you sit down, Doctor?

Dr Parry No thank you. I prefer to stand.

Rose (*teasing*) The judge always maintains an elevated position. The suspects cower below him.

Mavis Rose dear, this is serious.

Dr Parry (*clearing his throat and taking up a commanding position*) It seems to me that one important feature of the mystery is the conversation about death, which took place here this morning. The idea of the old man with the scythe must have sprung from that, don't you agree?

They nod and murmur assent

So let's recall who was present at the time, apart from the old lady herself.

Sylvia There was Rose and myself—and Arthur—and Ellen.

Ellen *I* wasn't there. I was out in the kitchen slicing beans.

Rose (*teasing*) I bet you weren't. I bet you were outside the door, listening with all your ears.

Ellen Rose, you're mean. I wish I'd never *told* you what I saw through the window.

Mavis (*drily*) I'm sure we all wish that; Ellen, but we can't turn back the clock.

Rose The moving finger writes ...

Dr Parry Now, out of those three people ... possibly four ...

Ellen glares at him

... which one had a motive, any motive, for harming Mrs Bell?

Rose Why, Arthur Fox did, of course. The strongest possible motive. He discovered only this morning ...

Sylvia (*warningly*) Rose!

Rose stops and looks doubtfully at Mavis

Mavis What did he discover?

Rose (*to Sylvia*) Mother, she's got to know. Please tell her. Dr Parry is very
   discreet.
Sylvia Ellen isn't.
Rose Ellen probably knows already. The beans were very badly sliced.

*Rose and Ellen make a face at each other. Sylvia goes and sits by Mavis and
takes her hand*

Sylvia Mavis dear . . . twenty years ago, when Arthur and you were such
   friends, we all expected him to marry you. We none of us understood why
   he suddenly went away without a word of explanation. But this morning
   we discovered that Mother told him you were engaged to someone else.
   He was very hurt and he left without seeing you again . . .
Mavis (*stunned*) Mother did what?
Sylvia She told him you were engaged to someone else.
Mavis (*quietly*) So that was it. I might have guessed.
Sylvia Please try to forgive her, dear. It was a long time ago.
Mavis And Arthur found out today that it wasn't true?
Rose Yes, and he was livid. He stormed out in a temper, shouting "Your
   grandmother hasn't heard the last of this!"
Mavis Poor Arthur. It must have been quite a shock.
Rose But don't you see, he had the motive. He was heard to utter threats.
Sylvia That's right, he did have a motive.

They look at Dr Parry expectantly

Dr Parry Is Arthur Fox a middle-aged man with a strong Yorkshire accent
   and a cheerful taste in neckties?
Rose Yes. Why? Have you met him?
Dr Parry Yes, in my surgery this afternoon. He had fallen down some steps
   and sprained his ankle and I bandaged it up for him. (*Pause*) He left my
   surgery about half past five.
Rose (*deflated*) The perfect alibi.
Dr Parry I'm afraid so. You can cross Mr Fox off the list.
Rose But I felt positive it must be him. No-one else had such a strong need
   for revenge. If you had seen his face when he left this room . . .
Ellen Which way did he go?
Rose I think he went out the back way.
Ellen Then he saw the scythe in the porch.
Dr Parry It doesn't matter what he saw, he was in my surgery when it
   happened and you can't get round that.
Rose He could have paid someone else to do it while he fixed himself an
   alibi.
Dr Parry Are you seriously suggesting that he deliberately sprained his
   ankle?
Rose Are you sure he wasn't foxing?

Ellen goes off into a fit of giggles and Rose smiles too

   I mean, was it a real, bona fide sprain?
Dr Parry (*smiling*) Yes, swollen up like a pudding. He wasn't foxing. No,

we haven't solved the mystery yet. We must plough on with the questions.

Rose Must we? If Arthur's out of the running, I don't think I'm going to like the alternative.

Dr Parry Where were you, Miss Rose, when the event took place?

Rose Up in my bedroom, sulking.

Dr Parry Sulking?

Rose All right, crying. I'd had a row with Grandma. She spilled medicine all over the shawl I'd made for her.

Mavis Oh, dear.

Dr Parry Can you tell me what you did when you heard her scream?

Rose I ran downstairs and found her lying here on the floor.

Dr Parry Was your mother not with her?

Rose No. She came in later.

Dr Parry How much later?

Rose A few minutes. I can't be sure.

Dr Parry Where was the clothes horse?

Rose In the middle of the room.

Dr Parry Was the black cloak on it?

Rose Er ... I think so.

Dr Parry And one stocking?

Rose I don't know.

Dr Parry (*to Sylvia*) Mrs Morley, you were the last person to see your mother before the ... er ... apparition. What happened?

Sylvia She was complaining about her heart. The medicine you gave her had been spilled——

Rose On my shawl.

Sylvia —So I had to go and find her pills.

Dr Parry How long were you gone?

Sylvia About five minutes. It took quite a time because she had pushed them to the very back of the cupboard among a lot of other pill boxes. There were dozens of them and they all looked the same. I had taken off the lid of a box to see if they were the right ones and then, suddenly, I heard her scream very loudly.

Dr Parry You were upstairs?

Sylvia No, Mother's room is just across the hall. When she screamed, my hand jerked and all the pills fell out on the floor. I began to run to Mother and I must have trodden on the pills because my feet just went from under me. I fell down with a bang and hit my head on the end of the bedstead. I was quite dizzy for a few moments. Then I pulled myself together and ran in here and found Rose rubbing Mother's hands and Ellen putting a cushion under ...

Mavis Ellen? I thought she was outside the window.

Ellen No, I came in. I could tell something was very wrong and I ran to the back door and found it unlocked so I rushed straight in to see if I could help.

Dr Parry When you came through the porch, was the scythe back in place?

Ellen I've no idea. I didn't look.

Mavis I consider the girl's presence, inside or out, to be highly suspicious.

Are we supposed to believe that she set out in the tail end of a thunderstorm to deliver a gift to Rose ... (*She picks up the gift from sideboard*) a gift she hadn't bothered to wrap up properly nor even removed the price ... and just *happened* to glue her nose to the window at the precise moment when this hooded figure appeared? It's all highly unlikely. It's far more probable that she was the instigator of the whole affair. It's just the sort of trick she'd play. She's thoroughly childish.

Ellen I'm *not* childish.

Rose Aren't you? Who carries a toy cat around with her?

Rose picks up the toy cat and waves its paw

Miaow!

Ellen (*abashed*) That's a different kind of childish. I carry Felix around because he's someone to talk to when I'm feeling lonely. I cuddle him when I'm unhappy. Mother won't let me have a real pet so I pretend. It *is* childish and it's time I grew out of it. But that doesn't mean I'd play a silly trick for no reason ...

Dr Parry No, Ellen had no motive to harm Mrs Bell.

Mavis Ellen doesn't need a motive. When she's bored, she'd do anything for a bit of excitement.

Ellen That's a wicked thing to say! If anyone has a motive, it's *you*, Miss Bell.

Mavis What d'you mean?

Ellen I know how she treated you. How she bullied you and made you cry. How she pretended you'd robbed her ...

Dr Parry That's quite enough of that, Ellen. Miss Bell wasn't back from Cheltenham at the time.

Ellen At what time?

Dr Parry About five fifteen. Her train didn't get in until five thirty.

Ellen She could have come on an earlier train. There's one gets in about three o'clock.

Sylvia And hid herself away until five fifteen? How ridiculous. And anyway, Mavis didn't hear the conversation about the old man with the scythe.

Ellen Well, no ... but she said she'd often heard her mother make that joke, about sending a *young* man to get her.

Sylvia I never heard anything so far-fetched. Mavis *loves* Mother.

Ellen Oh does she? Then why did she tamper with her chair?

Sylvia What are you talking about?

Ellen That chair. I sat on it this morning and it collapsed.

Rose It didn't. It just sagged a bit.

Ellen It was *meant* to collapse. Someone had tampered with it so that Mrs Bell would get a nasty jolt. No-one else sits in that chair, do they?

Dr Parry Look, I mended that chair this morning and I saw no evidence that it had been tampered with. A castor had fallen off, that's all.

Ellen Castors don't fall off by accident.

Mavis Ellen, I assure you that I have never tampered with Mother's chair. And as for your suggestion that I was the hooded figure, I think I can prove that I wasn't, if I may just fetch something from my room.

Mavis exits

Dr Parry (*thoughtfully*) I suppose it's just possible that she could have come on an earlier train . . . walked up from the station . . .

Rose Dr Parry! How could you even *consider* such a possibility? Aunt Mavis is the last person . . .

Dr Parry I know. I wouldn't give it another thought only . . . your grandmother said something.

Rose When?

Dr Parry When I was getting her to sleep, just now.

Rose What did she say?

Dr Parry It was very indistinct. She was half asleep. It sounded like, "The maiden shouldn't have been there".

Rose "The maiden shouldn't have been there"?

Dr Parry Yes. Or something very similar. And I have heard Mrs Bell call her daughter names like that . . . "old maid", "Maiden aunt" . . .

Rose Aren't you jumping to conclusions, Dr Parry? There are two other maidens in this case, Ellen and me.

Sylvia And Ellen *certainly* shouldn't have been there.

Ellen I wasn't. I came in afterwards, didn't I, Rose?

Rose That doesn't prove you hadn't been in already.

Dr Parry It seemed such an odd expression.

Sylvia I don't think so. Village people often call girls "maidens".

Rose Grandmother used to talk about maidenhood as if it was some dreadful incurable disease.

Sylvia Rose, don't talk about her in the past tense. She's still alive, you know.

Mavis enters carrying a newspaper

Mavis Here you are, Dr Parry. The *Cheltenham Evening News*. It has, today's date. I bought it on Cheltenham station at four o'clock. How could I have bought that if I had travelled on an earlier train?

Dr Parry Four o'clock? Yes, that's about the time it gets on to the streets. You certainly couldn't have obtained it two hours earlier. Look, Ellen, this proves you wrong, doesn't it? (*He hands paper to Ellen*)

Rose And if you're going to make stupid accusations against my aunt, who has never done you the slightest harm, you can keep your rotten present. I don't want it.

Ellen subsides, scowling

Mavis Well, we don't seem much nearer a solution, do we? Don't you think we could stop this probing, Doctor?

Dr Parry It's true, I'm not a very good investigator. If I could be sure it was nothing but a childish prank, I wouldn't worry so much. But the possibility that it was done with malicious intent, to frighten an old lady into her grave, is something I can't overlook. (*Pause*) Could we just go over the timing? I feel that it's important. You see . . . it had to be done so quickly. Whoever it was had to get the scythe from the porch, sneak in and get the cloak and stocking, put them on, frighten the old lady, take them off and return them to their proper place, take back the scythe, all in the space of five minutes. You *were* gone about five minutes, weren't you, Mrs Morley?

Sylvia Er . . . yes. About that long.

Dr Parry It was obviously something done on an impulse. No-one could plan those circumstances. (*Pause*) Miss Rose, you're not wearing your spectacles?

Rose No. I was crying, you see. You can't cry with glasses on.

Dr Parry True. (*Challengingly*) And you can't put a stocking over your head, either.

Rose stares at him for a moment, in silence. Then she shrugs and laughs

Rose All right. Let's not prolong the agony any longer. I did it.

Mavis } *together* { You!
Ellen

Rose Yes, of course it was me. I was furious with her for spoiling my shawl. I decided to pay her out. Of course I only meant to frighten her. It was just a childish prank, as you said.

Mavis Rose! I can't believe it of you.

Rose Can't you, Auntie? No, you don't know me very well. You see, I'm not such a saint as you. When someone spites me, I hit back.

Dr Parry (*incredulously*) And you did this—this unkind trick on a helpless old lady, just because she accidentally ruined a shawl?

Rose Dr Parry, I worked on that shawl for nearly a year. It was a beautiful work of art. The stitches were intricate and delicate. When I had finished it my eyes ached but I glowed with pride. Then my grandmother deliberately poured her entire bottle of medicine over it. Can't you understand how I felt?

Dr Parry No, I can't. Your grandmother would never do such a thing on purpose. I'm sorry, Miss Morley, but I thought better of you than that.

Rose (*turning away*) Then you have been misled.

Dr Parry (*after an uncomfortable pause*) I had better go. Good night, Mrs Morley, Miss Bell. I'll come and see your mother in the morning. Come along, Ellen. I'll see you home.

Ellen turns to go, then pauses, runs to Rose and kisses her

Ellen Good-bye, Rose. I understand, really I do.

Ellen and Dr Parry exit

There is a long silence in the parlour. Then Sylvia bursts into tears and buries her face in her hands. Mavis goes and kneels by her

Mavis Don't cry, Sylvia. It's not so terrible, really. Just a childish joke. After all, she was greatly provoked, weren't you, Rose?

Rose Greatly.

Sylvia You don't understand, Mavis. It wasn't Rose.

Rose Mother, please, don't go on.

Sylvia I must. I can't let you take the blame for me. It's so unfair that everyone should blame you when you're innocent.

Mavis Rose is innocent?

Sylvia Of course she is.

Mavis Then ... why did you say it was you, Rose?

Rose It was pretty clear that Dr Parry had narrowed down the field to the two of us. I thought I'd better confess before he started questioning Mother.

Sylvia (*to Rose*) You knew it was me all along, didn't you?

Rose Not at first. Then I remembered that when I came down and found Grandma unconscious, Ellen was the first to appear and then you came running in ... but instead of hurrying to Grandma's side, you stopped a moment to straighten the black cloak on the clothes horse. Also your hair was very untidy. You'd had no time to comb it after removing the stocking.

Mavis But I don't understand. You're the last person to want to play a trick on Mother.

Sylvia It wasn't a trick, Mavis.

Mavis It wasn't?

Sylvia No. I meant it to be fatal. *I wanted her dead! I wanted her dead!*

Rose (*putting her arms round her*) Hush, Mother, hush!

Sylvia It was for your sake I did it, Mavis.

Mavis For my sake?

Sylvia And to ease my dreadful guilty conscience about you. Oh Mavis, I did a terrible thing twenty years ago and I never realized until today what I'd done to you.

Mavis My dear, you're not talking sense. You're over-wrought. Rose, please get her a glass of wine.

Rose does so

Now Sylvia, blow your nose and say nothing until you've got that wine inside you.

Sylvia sips and calms down a little

That's right, and in a minute you shall tell us all about it. As Rose says, "confession is good for the soul".

Sylvia has some more wine and wipes her eyes

Sylvia Twenty years ago I was twenty-two and very much in love. Peter Morley had asked me to marry him. He had a good job waiting for him in Ceylon and I had only to name the day, but I held back because of Arthur Fox.

Mavis Because of Arthur?

Sylvia Yes. He was your sweetheart and we all hoped that you would marry him. I must confess I didn't like him very much but that didn't matter so long as you loved him. You were thirty years old and I thought of him as your last chance.

Mavis You were probably right.

Sylvia One half of me wanted you to marry him. The other half of me dreaded it.

Mavis Dreaded it?

Sylvia Oh yes, don't you see? It was obvious that whichever of us married first, the other sister would have to stay at home and look after Mother. Father was dead. She was already a semi-invalid and beginning to depend on us for everything. I began to hate the sight of Arthur Fox ... but I couldn't bring myself to make my wedding plans. Then one day, Arthur didn't turn up. He never came near or wrote a letter ... do you remember?

Mavis (*dryly*) I remember.

Sylvia You looked so pale and miserable and you never said a word. I just held my breath, hoping, fearing, hating myself all the time. I even *prayed* that he would never come back. Wasn't that terrible of me? I waited three months, Mavis—then I married Peter and went off to Ceylon. If we'd stayed in England I might have helped you, but I went off to Ceylon and left you tied to Mother, hand and foot.

Mavis Of course you did. Why ever not? I was very happy for you.

Sylvia I know. And you wrote such cheerful letters and I never guessed what life was like for you until this week, when I had to be servant and cook and nurse and companion with never a moment to call my soul my own. Then, today, Mother admitted to me it was *she* who sent Arthur away. That she told him you were engaged to someone else and he walked out of your life. And I realized that, but for her, our lives would have been reversed. You would have been the happily married woman, with children of your own. I would have been the household drudge. I was so *ashamed*, Mavis.

Mavis You had no cause.

Sylvia So ashamed and so guilty and so angry that she could do that to you and get away with it. I wanted her to die.

Rose I can guess what you felt like.

Sylvia Not just because she deserved to be punished—which she did—but because she might, by her death, have set things right. Arthur Fox is a widower now. He came here to look for you. If only Mother had died, you'd have been free to marry him.

Mavis *Marry* him!

Sylvia You're only fifty. Lots of women marry late in life and find great happiness. But it didn't work. I'm sorry, Mavis. I tried to put things right for you.

Mavis (*looking at her with compassion*) Poor Sylvia. You mustn't see yourself as the cause of my spinsterhood. You held back as long as a girl in love could possibly hold back. And I got over Arthur Fox within a year. I never loved him, you know.

Sylvia You did! You know you did!

Mavis No. I would have married him because he was kind and good-tempered and I would have had a home and children, but I never loved him. Who knows, I might even have grown to hate him. But now that I'm too old to have children and too settled to leave this place, I would *never* consider being Arthur Fox's second wife. No, I shall carry on, just as I always have, caring for Mother until she dies . . . going off to Cheltenham once a year . . .

Rose Oh Auntie, it sounds so dull.

Mavis It will be far better now that you and your mother will be living nearer. Perhaps you'll come and visit me again?

Rose Of course I will. I'll come on my own if Mother can't get away.

Mavis Sylvia, what time is the cab coming to take you to the station?

Sylvia Eight o'clock. Goodness, I haven't finished packing.

Rose I'll do that, Mother. You go and help Auntie make us all a cup of tea. I'm sure that's what we need.

Mavis Don't forget your stockings, dear.

Sylvia And Ellen's notepaper. Shall you write to her?

Rose Oh yes. She'll keep me up to date with all the village gossip.

Mavis I'm afraid that once you and Sylvia have left, nothing exciting is likely to happen.

Mavis exits

Rose I can't help hoping she's right.

Sylvia What do you mean by that?

Rose I don't know. I've just got a sort of feeling . . . Mother, do we have to go and leave Aunt Mavis all alone?

Sylvia We must, dear. Daddy's meeting the train. It's too late to change our plans now.

Rose (*deep in thought*) What do you think Grandma meant when she said "The maiden shouldn't be there."?

Sylvia Goodness knows. I very much doubt if that's what she really said. Dr Parry admits he may have been mistaken. Come along, dear, it's getting late.

Sylvia exits

When she is alone, Rose goes to Mrs Bell's chair and turns it over. She kneels down and examines it closely with an anxious frown

Sylvia (*off*) Rose?

Rose Coming!

Looking worried, Rose rights the chair and hurries out

The lights dim. When they come up again it is an hour later. The stage is empty. The front door bell rings. Mavis goes across the hall to the door

Mavis (*off*) Dr Parry!

Dr Parry (*off*) Forgive me for disturbing you. May I come in for a moment?

Mavis (*off*) Of course. Come into the parlour.

Mavis enters, followed by Dr Parry

Mother is still sleeping. I look in on her every ten minutes or so.

Dr Parry You are very good to her. Your sister and niece have gone I take it?

Mavis Yes. They had to catch the eight-thirty train to London. I was sorry to see them go. They were such good company.

Dr Parry Yes. A charming pair of ladies. (*Pause*) I was ... rather hard on Miss Rose, I'm afraid.

Mavis It was understandable, I suppose.

Dr Parry I had a very high opinion of her, you see. I thought she was so forthright and honest ... nothing coy or insincere about her. To play a trick on that old lady seemed so out of character.

Mavis hesitates, inclined to tell him the truth, but decides against it

Mavis We all do things that we are ashamed of afterwards. Impulsiveness is a fault but it is easily understood and forgiven, don't you agree?

Dr Parry (*heartily*) Oh indeed, yes. I'm sorry now that I parted with your niece on bad terms. Will she ... be coming again to visit you?

Mavis (*smiling*) Of course she will. She has promised to come again quite soon. Won't you sit down, Doctor? I'll just put the maiden out of sight.

The doctor is about to sit, but this remark jerks him upright

Dr Parry The what?

Mavis The maiden. It's a North-country word for the clothes horse. Quaint, isn't it?

She takes it out into the hall

Dr Parry Very quaint. And such a simple explanation.

Mavis re-enters and sits on the sofa

I've a letter for you. From Dr Thorne.

He hands her an envelope. Mavis stares at it blankly

Mavis A letter? But I only ... excuse me.

She opens it nervously, tries to read it but can't

I'm afraid I've left my spectacles with my luggage at the station. I wonder if you would be so kind as to read it to me.

Dr Parry (*embarrassed*) Oh, I couldn't do that, Miss Bell. A private letter. Please don't ask it of me.

Mavis (*quietly*) Dr Parry, you have been carrying letters between me and Dr Thorne for the past four years. You must have a pretty clear idea of what's going on.

Dr Parry It's none of my business. I don't wish to pry.

Mavis No-one could ever accuse you of prying. You've been the soul of discretion. But I've often wondered what you really thought about me. I'm not quite what you'd expect a scarlet woman to look like, am I? Fifty years old, plain and dowdy, not a thought in my mind but of works of charity ...

Dr Parry (*with a twinkle in his eye*) You look a very respectable lady.

Mavis I do, don't I? But *you* know I'm not.

Dr Parry I don't *know* anything. But I can't help noticing that every year, when you go on holiday to Cheltenham, Dr Thorne goes off to a week's conference at Gloucester. There must be a connection.

Mavis Of course there is. Just for one blissful week we are two different people. We book in at the hotel as Mr and Mrs Brown. He forgets all the worries and responsibilities of his practice. I forget the dreary monotony of life with Mother. You look astounded, Dr Parry. Are you very shocked?

Dr Parry I don't know *what* I am. You take my breath away. No, I don't think that I'm shocked. I think I'm glad that you have this . . . this joy in your life.

Mavis Yes. If it were not for this joy in my life I don't think I could carry on. It gives me a sort of inner strength. Of course, we have to be very careful. We set off separately and we come home on different trains. When we meet in the village we just nod and say "Good Morning" like chance acquaintances. Even the letters that you carry for us are limited to one a month. I wasn't expecting John to write to me so soon. It may be something important. Won't you please read it to me.?

Dr Parry I . . . well . . .

Mavis There'll be nothing embarrassing about it. It will start as it always starts, "My dear Mavis" and he will sign himself "Your loving friend, John".

Dr Parry Very well. (*He takes the letter and reads*) My dear Mavis, Our wonderful week has come and gone in a flash, leaving only a memory. The years that lie between these brief interludes of happiness are weary, frustrating and cruel. I think you know how it grieves me, to have you for only one week for my wife and then to part. It is almost worse than never having you at all. When I got home this afternoon there was a pile of letters waiting for me. One of them was very important to us both. My dear, I have been offered a post as Chief Medical Officer of Health in Edinburgh. Will you come with me as my wife? I have decided that if you will not come, I shall go alone. I cannot go on with this secret, hopeless affair. The loneliness is wearing me out. Better to break it off completely and say good-bye, try to forget you and make new friends. Believe me, I know what I am asking. I know so well how loyal and how indispensable you are to your mother. We cannot both have you. You must make a choice. I await your answer with much anxiety. Your loving friend, John."

Mavis sits as if turned to stone

Mavis (*after a moment*) This is the end, then.

Dr Parry It could be the beginning. Why shouldn't you marry him?

Mavis She'd never let me go.

Dr Parry Surely something could be arranged? Now your sister has returned to England?

Mavis She'll never let me go, I tell you. Never. You don't understand.

Dr Parry I'm sure she wouldn't wish to stand in your way.

Mavis Wouldn't she? You heard what she did years ago.

Dr Parry At least *try*. Don't turn Dr Thorne down without a try, *please*. It's only fair to him. (*Pause*) In the morning, if your mother is feeling better, you could show her this letter ...

Mavis Show her John's letter? Tell her how we've been deceiving her for years? Would that do her good?

Dr Parry No, you're right, of course. It's a difficult situation. No, don't say anything just yet. Another shock could be fatal. But perhaps in a few weeks' time, when she's fully recovered ...

Mavis (*abruptly, because she cannot hold back her tears much longer*) Tell Dr Thorne I will write to him in the morning. Good night, Dr Parry.

Dr Parry Good night, Miss Bell. I'll see myself out.

Dr Parry exits

Mavis stands listening till she hears the front door close. Then her sobs break out. In utter despair she throws herself on to the sofa, weeping on to the toy cat, then clutching it to her

Mavis John, John, I can't lose you. You're all I've got. (*After a while the sobs cease. She sits, looking down at the cat cradled in her arms. Slowly she rises and goes to the window, staring out unseeingly*) Another shock could be fatal. (*She looks down at the toy cat*) Another shock ...

A small hand bell rings

Mrs Bell (*off*) Mavis! Mavis!

Mavis hesitates, then, still nursing the cat, she goes out very quickly. After a moment she returns without the cat. She looks terrified. She shuts the door and leans against it

Mrs Bell (off) begins to scream

Mavis shuts her eyes tight and covers her ears with her hands

The screams dies away in a sobbing, gasping gurgle

CURTAIN

FURNITURE AND PROPERTY LIST

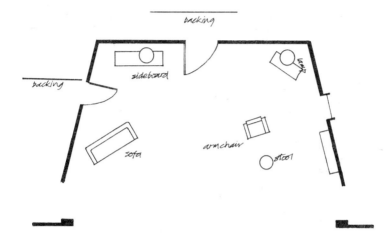

ACT I

SCENE 1

On stage: Fireplace. *Beside it:* clean shovel, grate-cleaning brush
Mantelpiece. *On it:* old cheap vase (to break) at one end, other objects
Sideboard. *On it:* bottle of pills and glass of water
Armchair
Sofa
Low stool
Curtains at windows (curtains open)
Two lamps
Other items of furniture to set the scene at the Producer's discretion

Off stage: Smelling salts **(Mrs Bell)**
Jewel-box containing "emerald" brooch **(Mavis)**
Wooden carving wrapped in paper **(Rose)**
Two shawls wrapped separately in paper **(Rose)**

Personal: **Ellen:** toy cat
Rose: spectacles

SCENE 2

Strike: Toy cat
        Pills
        Broken vase
        Wrapping paper
        Remove one castor from leg of chair

Off stage: Single size white sheet **(Sylvia)**
        Medicine in bottle **(Dr Parry)**
        Toolbox containing hammer, screwdriver and screws **(Ellen)**
        Warming pan **(Sylvia)**
        Picture postcard **(Ellen)**
        Brasso and cloth **(Rose)**
        Tray with wine decanter and four wine glasses **(Sylvia)**

Personal: **Rose:** grate-cleaning brush

SCENE 3

Strike: Medicine bottle
        Toolbox
        Warming pan
        Used glasses
        Brasso and cloth

Off stage: Medicine and spoon **(Sylvia)**
        Bag of buns **(Rose)**
        Purse with half-crown in it **(Rose)**
        Clothes horse with sheets **(Sylvia)**
        Scythe **(Sylvia)**

Personal: **Mrs Bell:** shawl
        Rose: black cloak

ACT II

Strike: Buns
        Purse
        Half-crown
        Shawl
        Medicine
        Scythe

Set: Curtains closed
        Toy cat on sofa
        Clean glasses on tray on sideboard
        Light two lamps
        Place folded clothes horse upstage with sheets, black cloak and one white
           stocking over it

Off stage: One crumpled white stocking **(Dr Parry)**
        Newspaper **(Mavis)**
        Letter from Dr Thorne **(Dr Parry)**

Personal: **Ellen:** small packet of stationery, unwrapped

LIGHTING PLOT

Interior of cottage. Practical fittings required: two oil lamps

Property fittings required: fire

ACT I, Scene 1.

To open: Afternoon sunshine through window and garden door

| *Cue* 1 | **Rose** exits | (Page 15) |
| | *Fade to Black-out* | |

ACT I, Scene 2.

To open: Morning sunshine

| *Cue* 2 | **Arthur** exits | (Page 25) |
| | *Fade to Black-out* | |

ACT I, Scene 3.

To open: Late afternoon, dull light. Firelight effect

Cue 3	**Sylvia** draws curtains	(Page 26)
	Darken room. Increase firelight effect	
Cue 4	**Sylvia** lights one lamp	(Page 26)
	Snap on covering light for lamp	
Cue 5	**Sylvia** exits with lamp	(Page 29)
	Darken room	
Cue 6	**Mrs Bell** falls to the floor	(Page 30)
	Fade to Black-out	

ACT II.

To open: Two lamps lit

Cue 7	**Sylvia** blows out the lamps	(Page 34)
	Extinguish covering spots	
Cue 8	**Rose** draws back curtains	(Page 34)
	Evening sunshine effect	
Cue 9	**Rose** hurries out	(Page 43)
	Lights dim and come up again to indicate passage of time	
Cue 10	**Mrs Bell's** screams die away	(Page 46)
	Fade to Black-out	

EFFECTS PLOT

ACT I

Cue 1   **Mrs Bell:** "Don't I get a kiss?" **Mavis:** "Of course."   (Page 5)
           Arrival of carriage

Cue 2   **Rose** cleans the grate   (Page 15)
           Door bell rings repeatedly

Cue 3   **Sylvia:** ". . . much difference, the way I make it."   (Page 17)
           Small hand bell rings off-stage

Cue 4   **Mrs Bell:** ". . . she let him slip through her fingers."   (Page 23)
           Door bell rings

Cue 5   **Arthur** exits   (Page 25)
           Door bangs off-stage

           To open Scene 3
Cue 6   *Rumble of thunder, heavy rain*   (Page 26)

Cue 7   **Mrs Bell:** ". . . having Arthur Fox for a son-in-law."   (Page 27)
           Door opens off-stage

ACT II

Cue 8   The lights dim. As they come up again   (Page 43)
           Door bell rings

Cue 9   **Mavis:** "Another shock."   (Page 46)
           Hand bell rings

MADE AND PRINTED IN GREAT BRITAIN BY
LATIMER TREND & COMPANY LTD PLYMOUTH

MADE IN ENGLAND